Just Gift It!

65

Plastic Canvas projects to make quick gifts

Table of Contents

Sailboat Tissue Box Cover

Size

4 1/2"w x 5 1/2"h x 4 1/2"d
(fits a 4 1/4"w x 5 1/4"h x 4 1/4"d boutique tissue box)

Supplies

Two 10 1/2" x 13 1/2" sheets of 7 mesh plastic canvas
Medium weight yarn
Embroidery floss
#16 tapestry needle

Stitches Used

Backstitch, Gobelin Stitch, Overcast Stitch, and Tent Stitch

Instructions

Follow charts to cut and stitch tissue box cover pieces. Use matching color Overcast Stitches for all joining. Matching long edges, join Sides. Join Top to Sides. For each Sail, match ♥'s, ★'s, and ◆'s; tack corners to Side #1.

Design by Conn Baker Gibney.

Color Key

- white
- yellow
- red
- lt blue
- dk blue
- green
- red (use 2 plies)
- white embroidery floss (use 6 strands)
- black embroidery floss (use 2 strands)
- metallic silver embroidery floss (use 6 strands)

Sail (24 x 28 threads) (stitch 2)

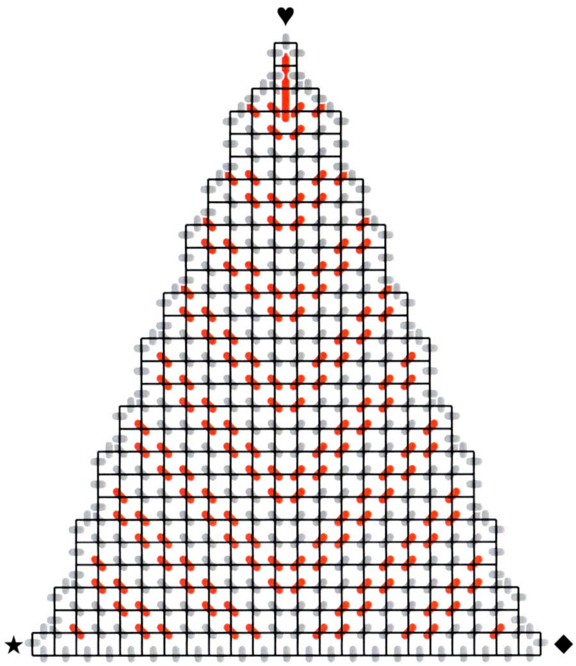

Top (32 x 32 threads)

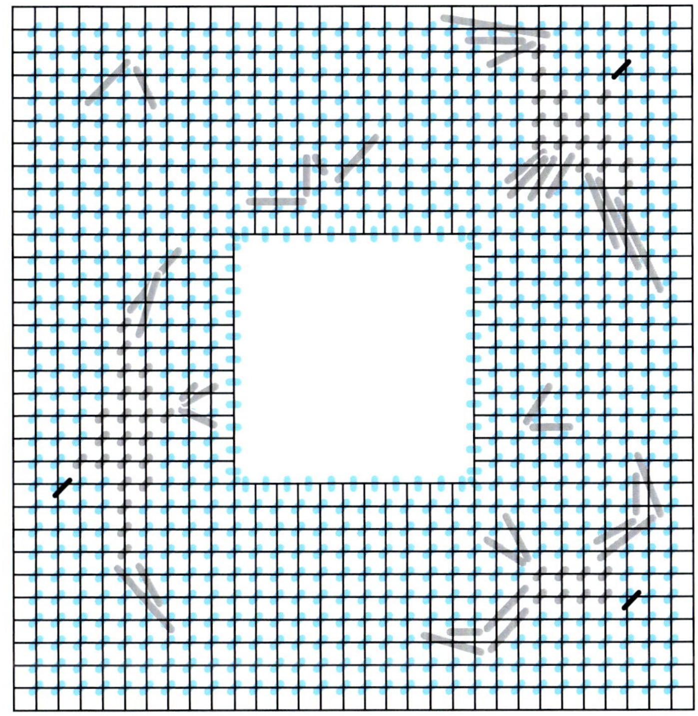

Side #1 (32 x 38 threads) (stitch 2)

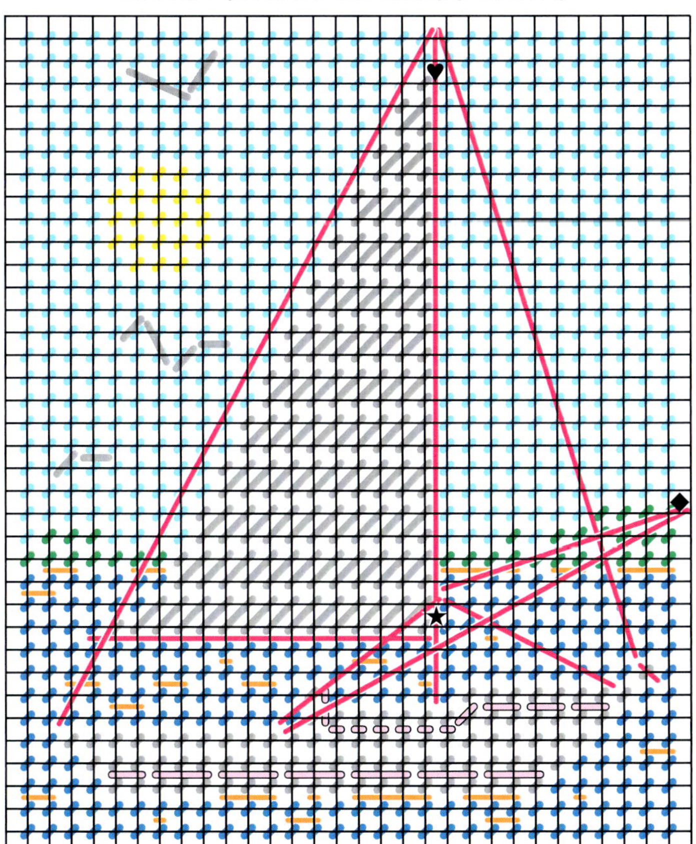

Side #2 (32 x 38 threads) (stitch 2)

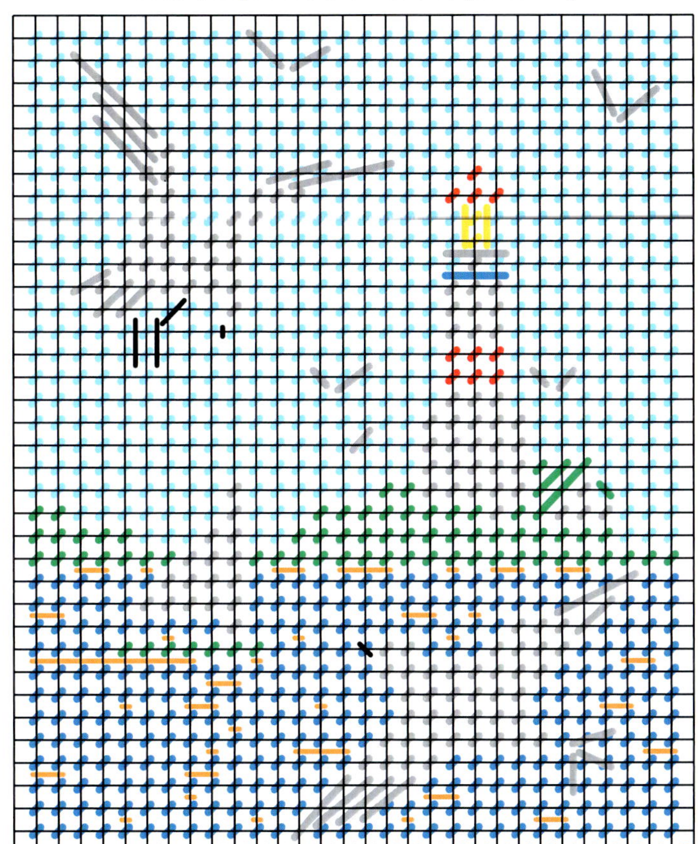

Kitty Coasters

Coaster Size
4 1/2"w x 3 1/4"h each

Holder Size
4 3/8"w x 1 1/4"h x 1 1/2"d

Supplies
- 10 1/2" x 13 1/2" sheets of 7 mesh plastic canvas
- Medium weight yarn
- #16 tapestry needle
- Cork or felt and craft glue (optional)

Stitches Used
Backstitch, Cross Stitch, Overcast Stitch and Tent Stitch

Instructions
Follow charts to cut and stitch Coaster set pieces. Matching ✖'s, use lt tan to join Side to Bottom. If backing is desired, cut cork or felt slight smaller than Coaster. Glue to back of Coaster.

Design by Sue Penrod.

Color Key
- lt tan
- black
- cat color

Cat Coaster (27 x 31 threads)

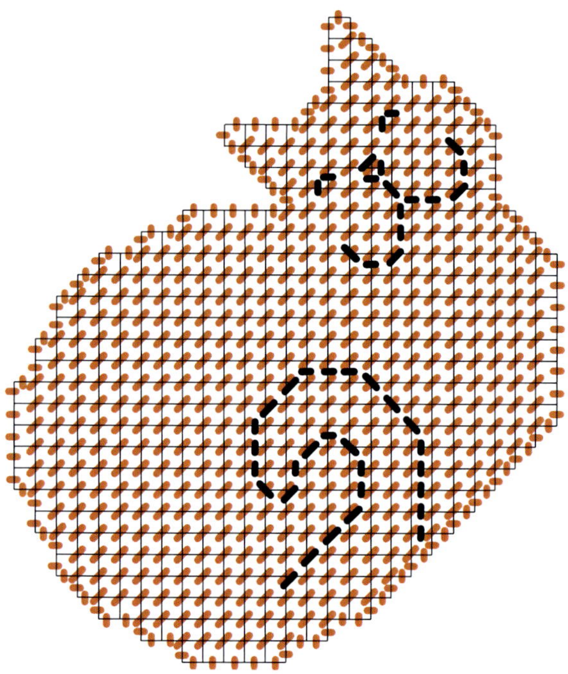

Bottom (27 x 9 threads)

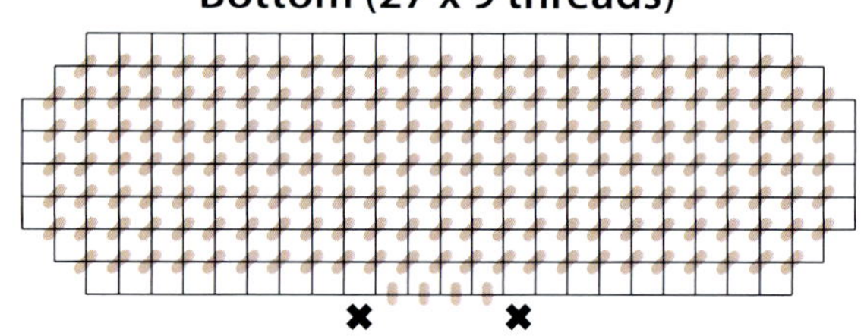

Side (62 x 8 threads)

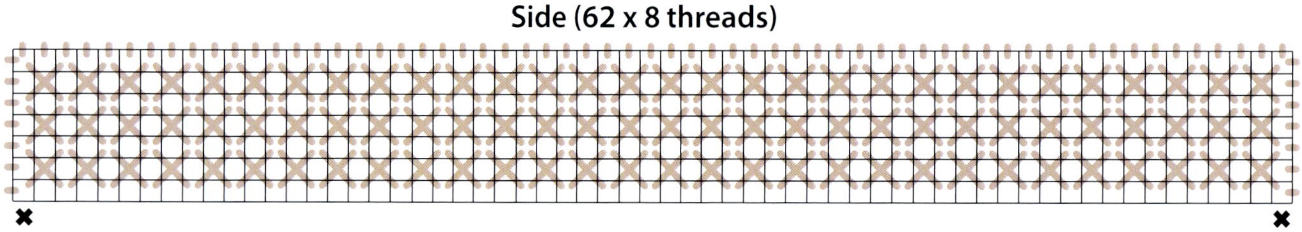

Flamingos Tissue Box Cover

Size

4 1/2"w x 5 1/2"h x 4 1/2"d
(fits a 4 1/4"w x 5 1/4"h x 4 1/4"d boutique tissue box)

Supplies

Two 10 1/2" x 13 1/2" sheets of 7 mesh plastic canvas
Medium weight yarn
Metallic blue yarn
Black embroidery floss
#16 tapestry needle

Stitches Used

Alternating Scotch Stitch, Backstitch, Double French Knot, Gobelin Stitch, Overcast Stitch, and Tent Stitch

Instructions

Follow charts to cut and stitch tissue box cover pieces. Use matching color Overcast Stitches for all joining. Matching long edges, join Sides. Join Top to Sides.

Design by Conn Baker Gibney.

Color Key

- white
- lt pink
- pink
- lt red
- lavender
- lt blue
- black
- metallic blue
- pink (use 2 plies of yarn)
- green (use 2 plies of yarn)
- black embroidery floss (use 6 strands)
- pink Double Fr. Knot

Top (32 x 32 threads)

Side #1 (32 x 38 threads) (stitch 2)

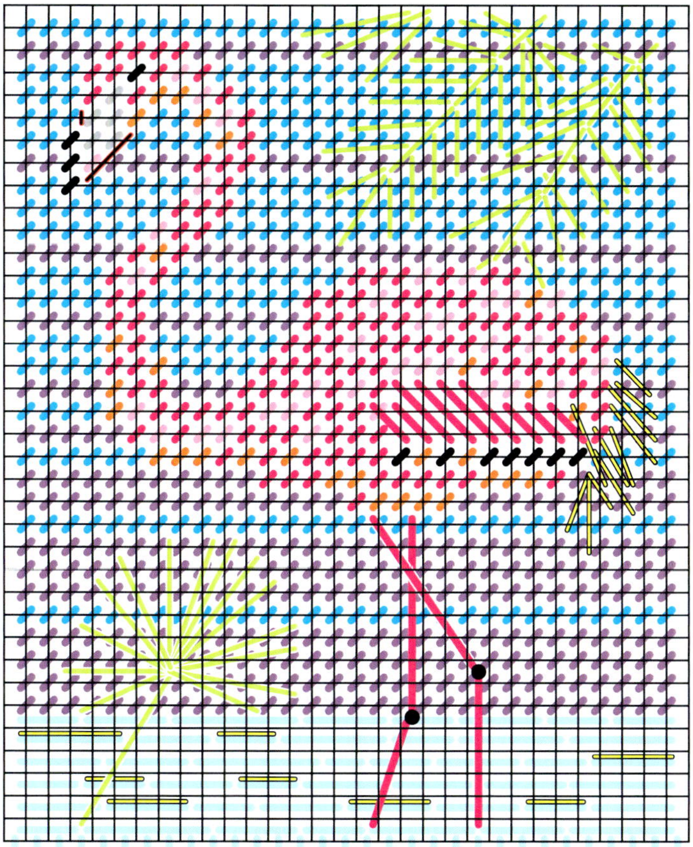

Side #2 (32 x 38 threads) (stitch 2)

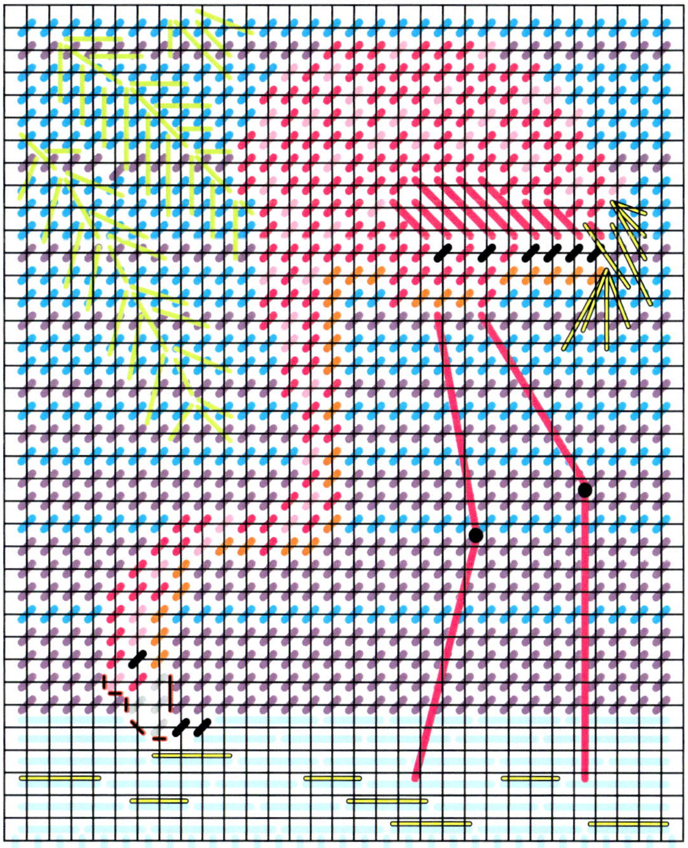

Home Sweet Home Tissue Box Cover

Size

4 1/2"w x 5 1/2"h x 4 1/2"d
(fits a 4 1/4"w x 5 1/4"h x 4 1/4"d boutique tissue box)

Supplies

Two 10 1/2" x 13 1/2" sheets of 7 mesh plastic canvas
Medium weight yarn
Embroidery floss
#16 tapestry needle

Stitches Used

Alternating Scotch Stitch, Backstitch, Cross Stitch, Gobelin Stitch, Overcast Stitch, and Tent Stitch

Instructions

Follow charts to cut and stitch tissue box cover pieces. Use matching color Overcast Stitches for all joining. Matching long edges, join Sides. Join Top to Sides.

Design by Conn Baker Gibney.

Top (32 x 32 threads)

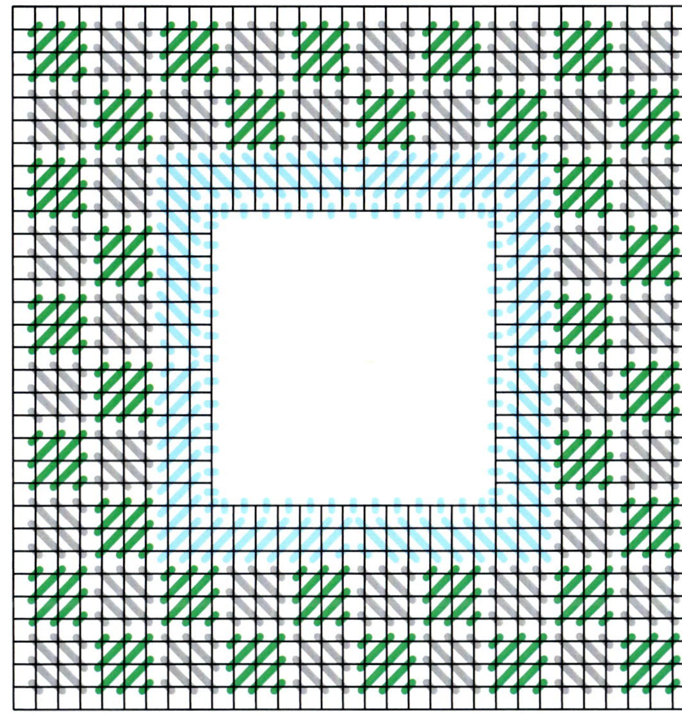

Side (32 x 38 threads) (stitch 4)

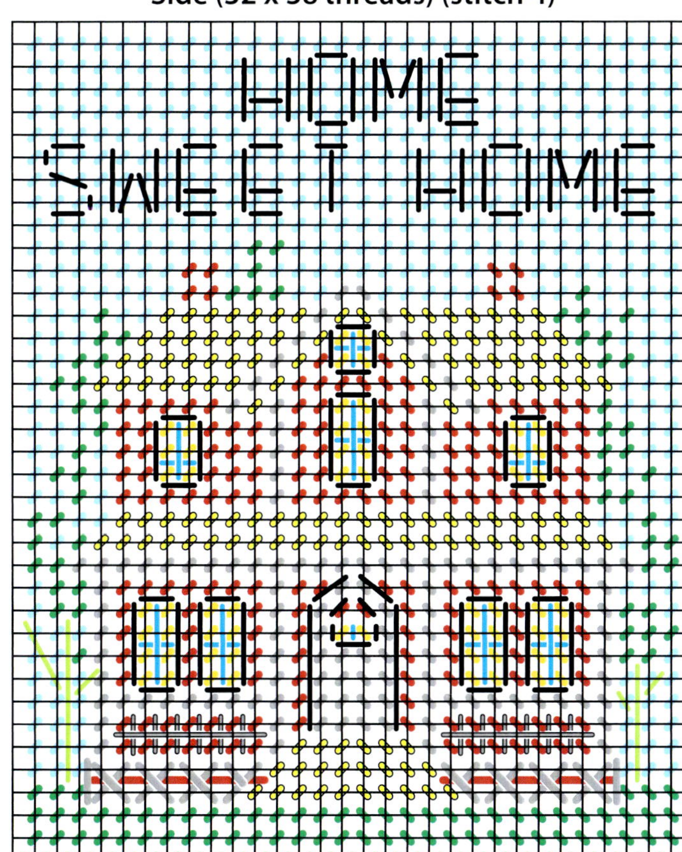

Color Key

- white
- yellow
- dk red
- lt blue
- green
- black
- white embroidery floss (use 6 strands)
- brown embroidery floss (use 6 strands)
- black embroidery floss (use 2 strands)
- black embroidery floss (use 6 strands)

Sunflower Coaster

Size
5 1/2"w x 5"h

Supplies
- 5" plastic canvas hexagon shape
- Medium weight yarn
- #16 tapestry needle
- Cork or felt and craft glue (optional)

Stitches Used
Backstitch, French Knot, Gobelin Stitch, Overcast Stitch, and Tent Stitch.

Instructions
Follow chart to stitch Coaster. If backing is desired, cut cork or felt slightly smaller than Coaster and glue to wrong side of Coaster.

Design by Ann Townsend.

Color Key

gold	blue
brown	dk blue
green	brown Fr. Knot

Coaster

Safari Coasters

Size

6"w x 3 1/2"h each

Supplies

- One 10 1/2" x 13 1/2" sheet of 7 mesh plastic canvas
- Medium weight yarn
- #16 tapestry needle
- Cork or felt and craft glue (optional)

Stitches Used

Fringe Stitch, Overcast Stitch, and Tent Stitch

Instructions

Follow chart to cut and stitch desired Coaster. Trim fringe stitches 3/4" from knot. If backing is desired, cut cork or felt slightly smaller than Coaster; glue to wrong side of Coaster.

Color Key

- white
- gold
- rust
- tan
- black
- gold Fringe
- black Fringe

Zebra Coaster (29 x 24 threads)

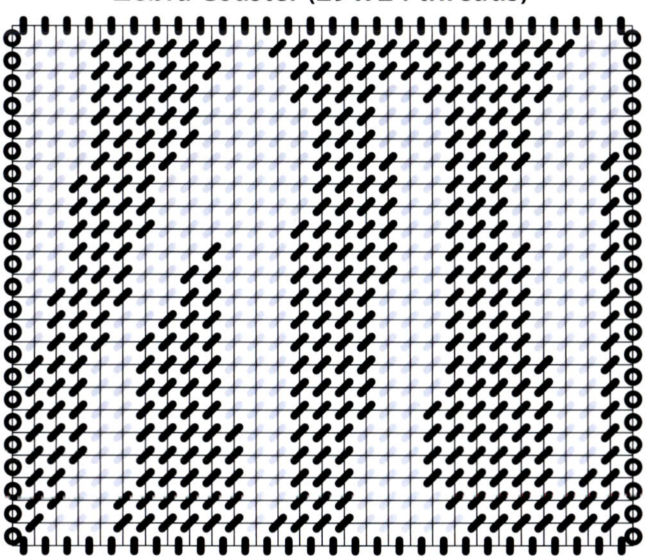

Giraffe Coaster (29 x 24 threads)

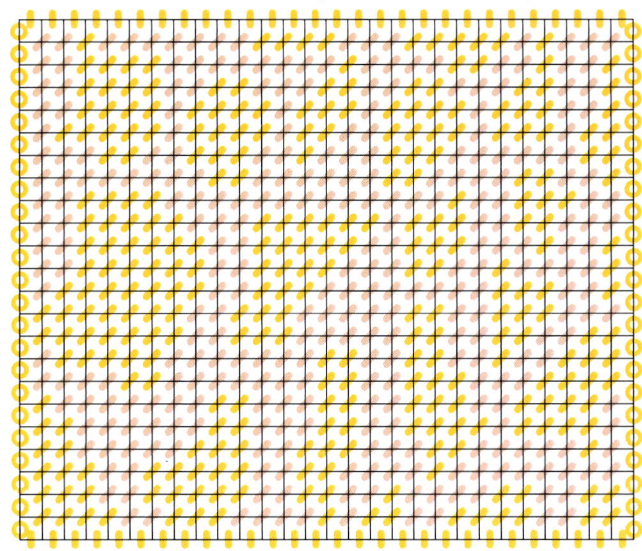

Tiger Coaster (29 x 24 threads)

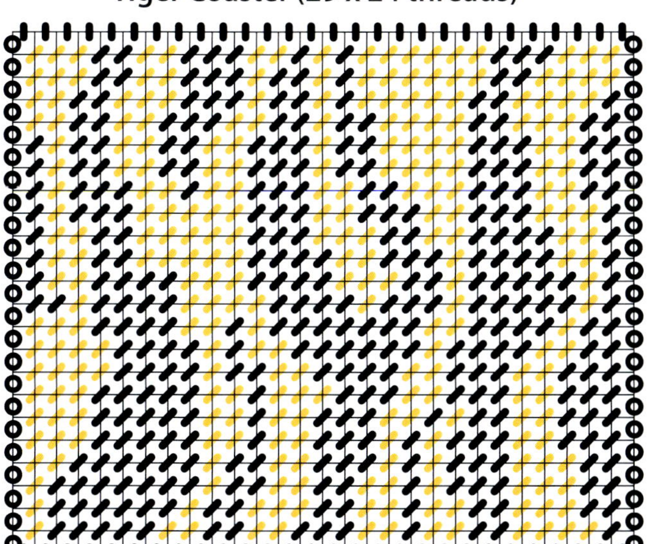

Leopard Coaster (29 x 24 threads)

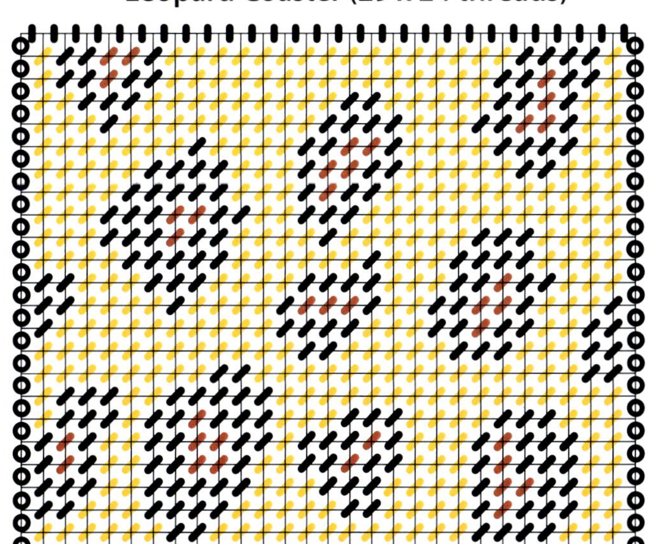

Beautiful Butterflies

Coaster Size
$4^{1}/_{8}$"w x $4^{1}/_{8}$"h each

Holder Size
$4^{7}/_{8}$"w x $4^{7}/_{8}$"h x $1^{3}/_{4}$"d

Supplies
- Three $10^{1}/_{2}$" x $13^{1}/_{2}$" sheets of 7 mesh plastic canvas
- Medium weight yarn and embroidery floss
- #16 tapestry needle
- Cork or felt and craft glue (optional)

Stitches Used
Backstitch, Cross Stitch, French Knot, Gobelin Stitch, Overcast Stitch, and Tent Stitch

Instructions
Use ecru for all joining and to cover unworked edges.

Follow charts to cut and stitch Butterfly Coasters Set, completing backgrounds as indicated on charts. Join Top Sides along short edges. Join Top to Top Sides.

For Bottom, cut a piece of canvas 30 x 30 threads. Bottom is not worked. Join Bottom Sides along short edges. Join Bottom to Bottom Sides. Cover unworked edges.

If backing for Coaster is desired, cut cork or felt slightly smaller than Coaster. Glue cork or felt to back of Coaster.

Designs by Kathleen Hurley.

Color Key

ecru	dk blue
lt yellow	vy lt green
yellow	lt green
vy lt orange	green
lt orange	dk green
orange	brown
dk orange	dk brown
lt violet	vy dk brown
violet	black
dk violet	*vy dk brown
vy lt blue	*vy dk brown French Knot
lt blue	*Use 3 strands of embroidery floss.
blue	

#1 (28 x 28 threads)

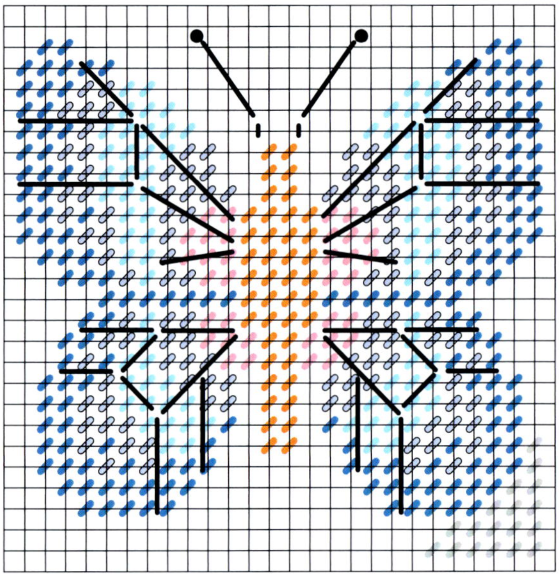

#2 (28 x 28 threads)

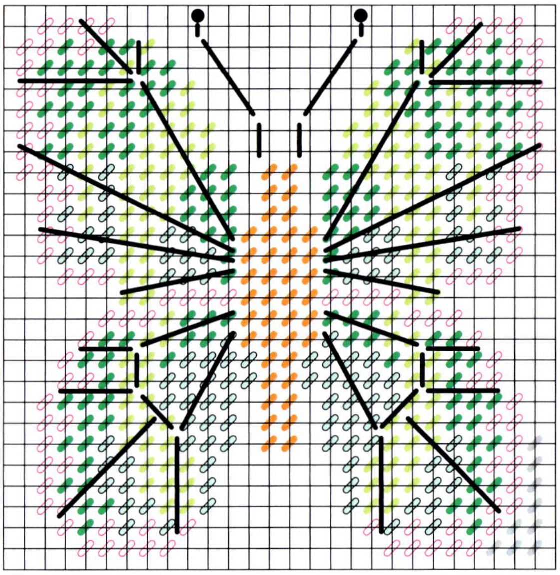

Top (32 x 32 threads)

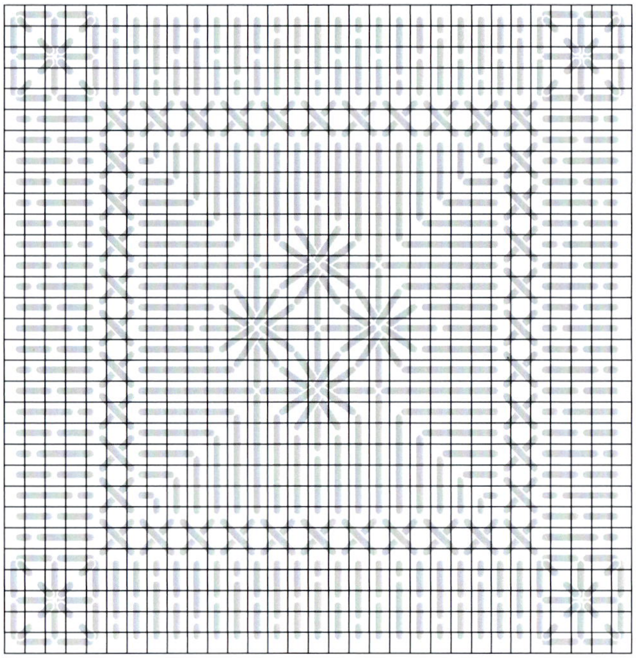

Top Side (32 x 6 threads) (stitch 4)

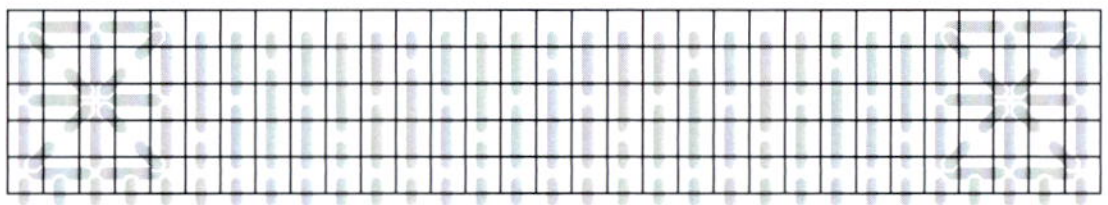

Bottom Side (30 x 16 threads) (stitch 4)

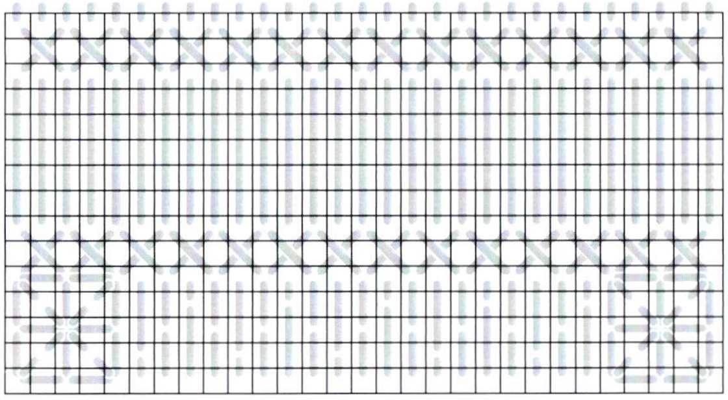

#3 (28 x 28 threads)

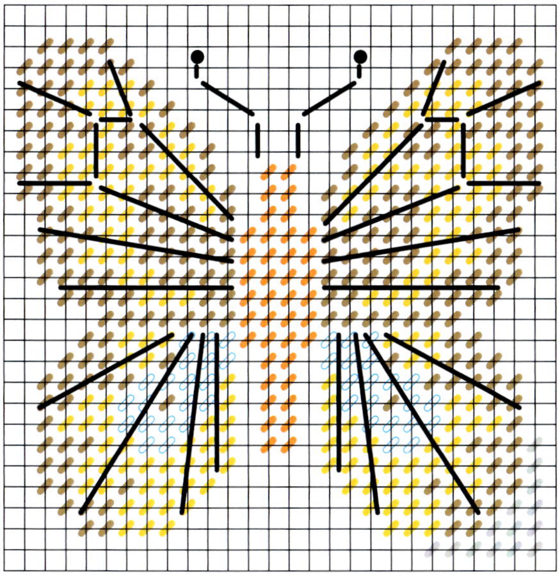

#6 (28 x 28 threads)

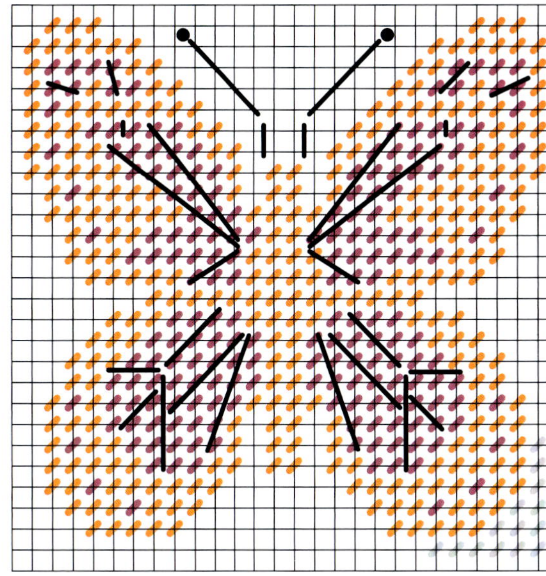

#4 (28 x 28 threads)

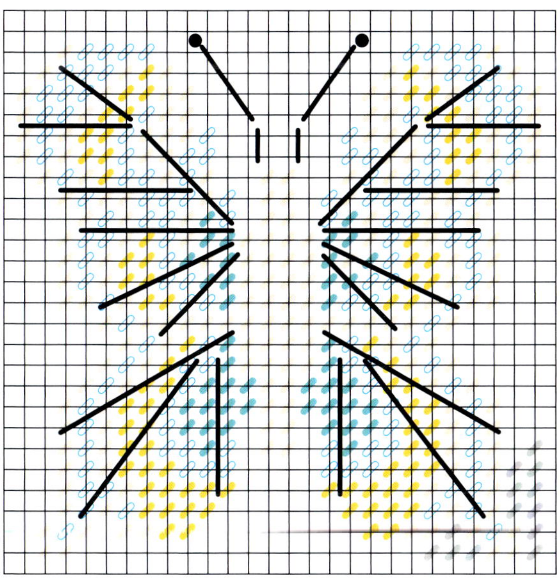

#7 (28 x 28 threads)

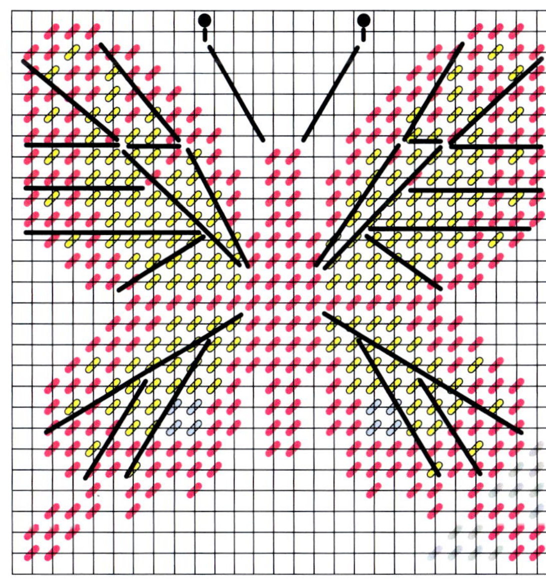

#5 (28 x 28 threads)

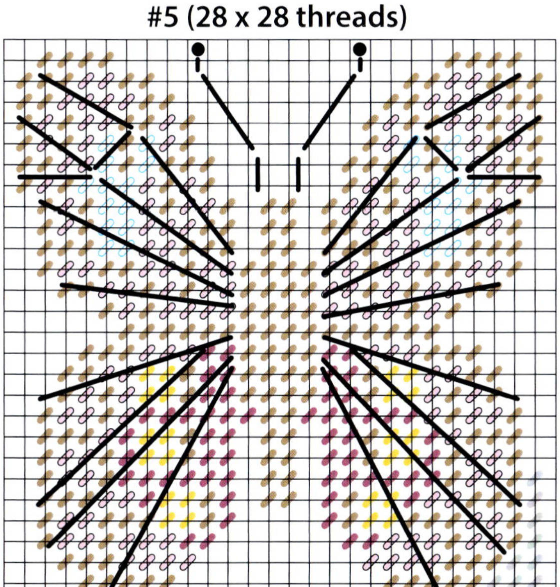

#8 (28 x 28 threads)

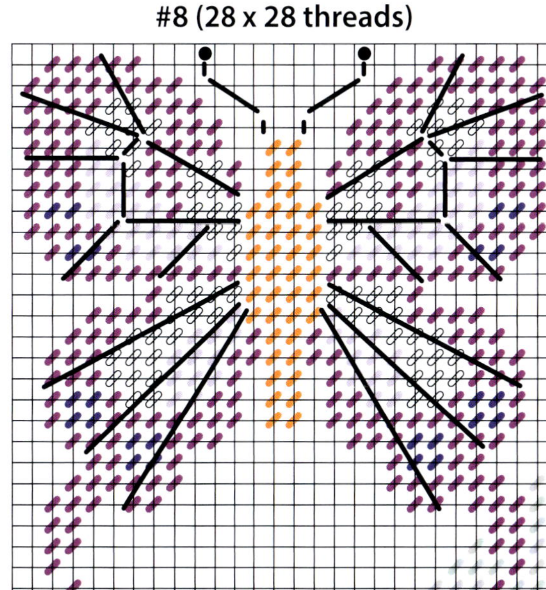

Make fruit sala
for potluck

Fruit Basket Favorites

Coaster Size

$4\frac{1}{2}$"w x $4\frac{1}{2}$"h each

Holder Size

$4\frac{3}{4}$"w x $7\frac{1}{2}$"h x $2\frac{1}{4}$"d

Magnet Size

$2\frac{1}{2}$"w x $2\frac{1}{2}$"h each

Supplies

Three $10\frac{1}{2}$" x $13\frac{1}{2}$" sheets of 7 mesh plastic canvas
One $8\frac{1}{2}$" x 11" sheet of 14 mesh plastic canvas
Medium weight yarn
Embroidery floss
#16 tapestry needle
#24 tapestry needle
24" length of $\frac{3}{8}$"w green grosgrain ribbon
magnetic strip
cork or felt (optional)
craft glue (optional)

Stitches Used

Backstitch, Cross Stitch, Gobelin Stitch, Lazy Daisy Stitch, Overcast Stitch, and Tent Stitch

Instructions

Use tan for all joining.

For Coaster Set, follow charts to cut and stitch Coaster Set pieces. For Bottom, cut a piece of plastic canvas 15 x 33 threads. Bottom is not worked. Matching ✖'s and ♥'s, join Sides to Front and Back. Join Bottom to Front, Back, and Sides. Matching ★'s, join Handle to Front and Back. If backing is desired, cut cork or felt slightly smaller than Coaster. Glue to back of Coaster.

For Magnets, cut and stitch the fruit pieces on 14 count perforated plastic using 6 strands of embroidery floss. Glue a magnet to back of Magnet.

Designs by Kathleen J. Fischer.

Color Key

white	dk pink	yellow green
yellow	red	dk yellow green
dk yellow	purple	tan
orange	dk purple	brown
dk orange	green	dk orange Lazy Daisy
pink	dk green	black Lazy Daisy

Lemon (33 x 25 threads)

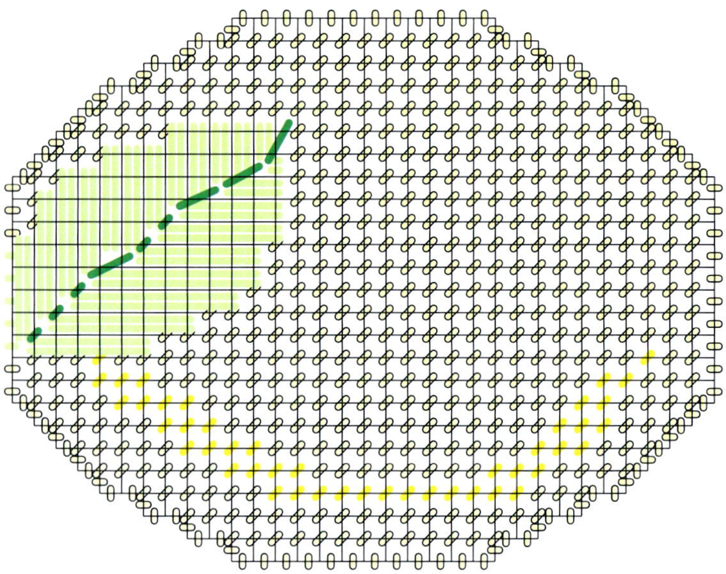

Watermelon (31 x 31 threads)

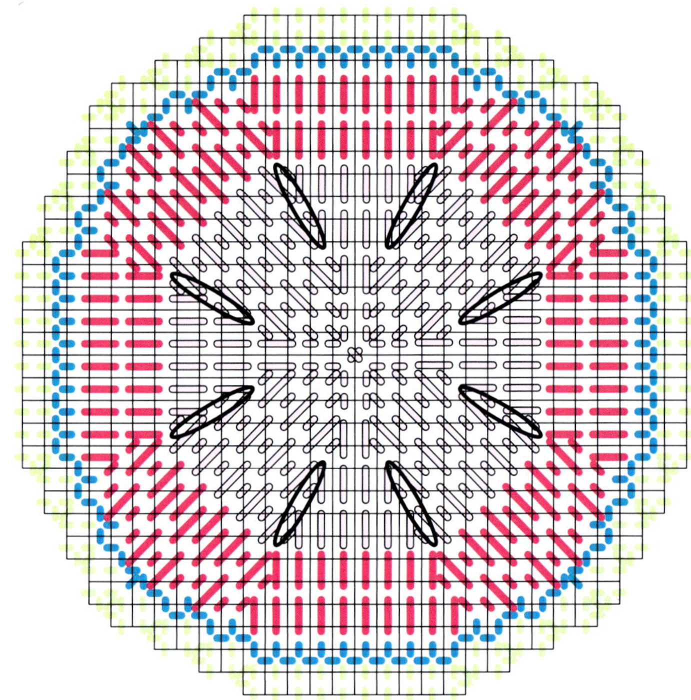

Grapes (32 x 34 threads)

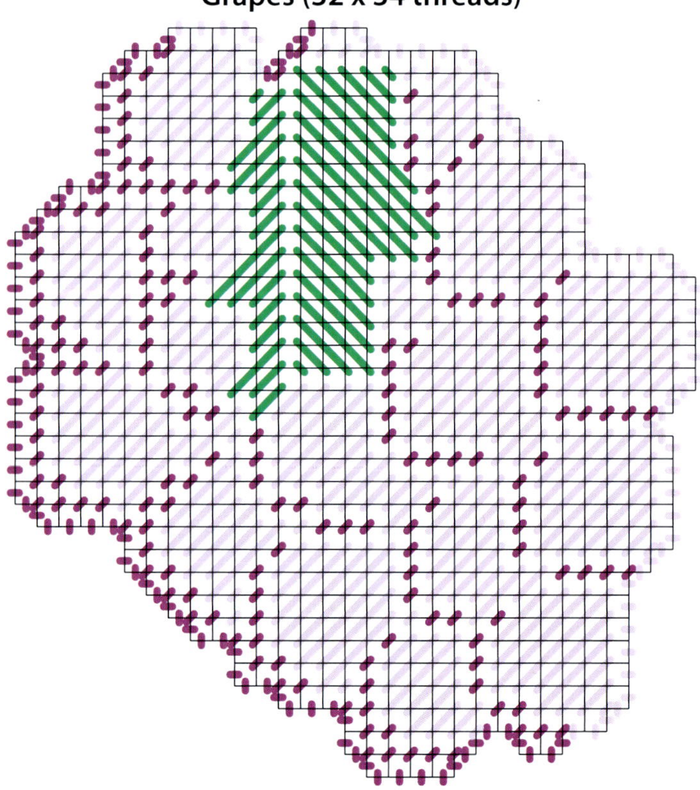

Orange (31 x 31 threads)

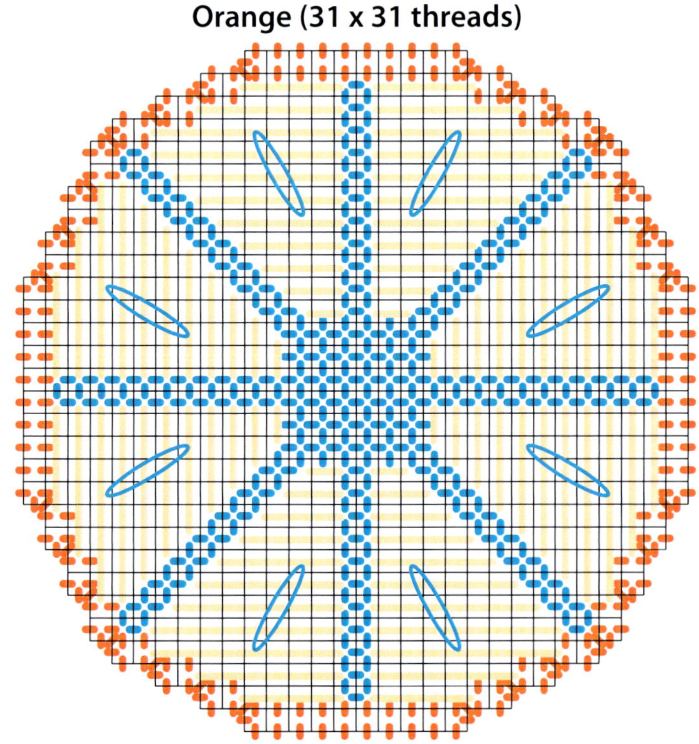

Apple (28 x 33 threads)

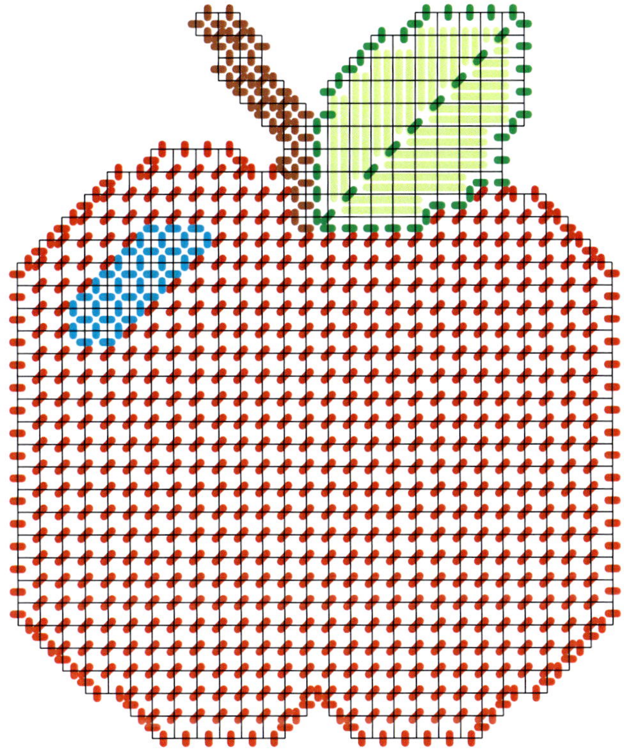

Handle (6 x 71 threads)

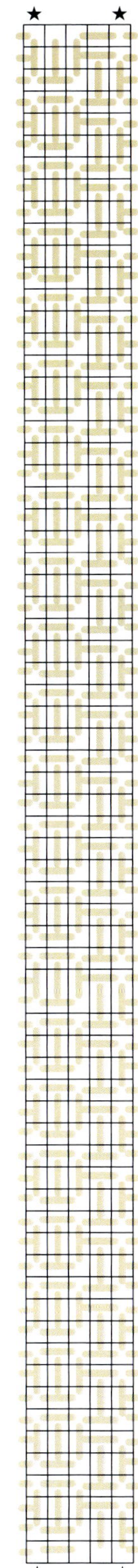

Pear (26 x 39 threads)

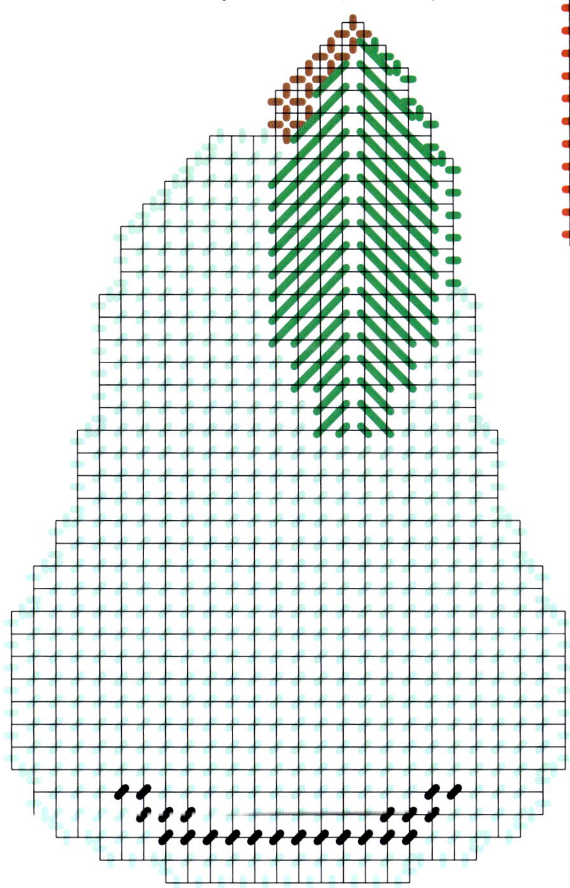

Side (15 x 22 threads) (stitch 2)

Front/Back (45 x 21 threads) (stitch 2)

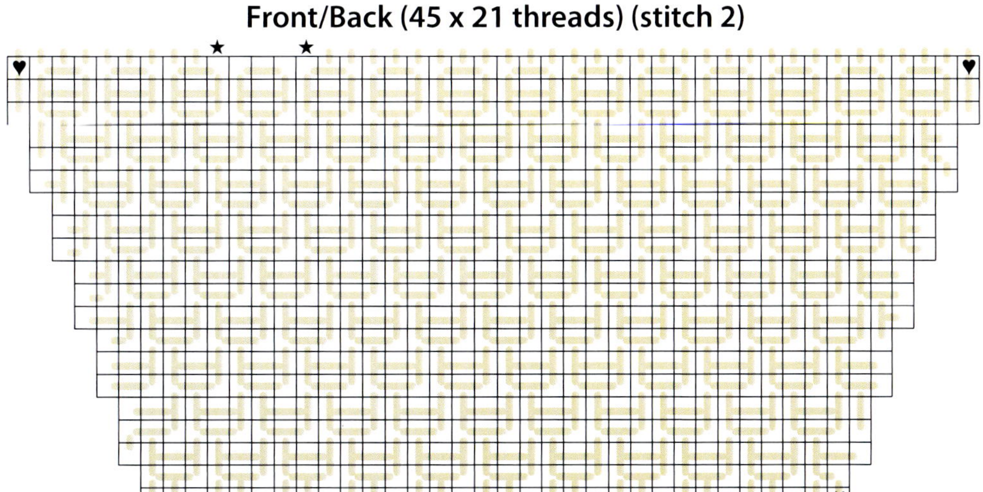

Size
$4^{1}/_{4}$"w x $4^{1}/_{4}$"h each

Supplies
One $10^{1}/_{2}$" x $13^{1}/_{2}$" sheet of 7 mesh plastic canvas
Medium weight yarn
#16 tapestry needle
Cork or felt and craft glue (optional)

Stitches Used
Backstitch, Overcast Stitch, and Tent Stitch

Instructions
Follow charts to cut and stitch Coasters, completing backgrounds as indicated on charts. If backing for Coaster is desired, cut cork or felt slightly smaller than Coaster. Glue to back of Coaster.

Designs by Kathleen Hurley.

Garden Fresh

Color Key

ecru	green
gold	dk green
lt orange	lt brown
orange	*lt brown
dk orange	brown
lt purple	dk brown
purple	*dk brown
blue	*uses 2 piles of yarn
lt green	

Beet Coaster (28 x 28 threads)

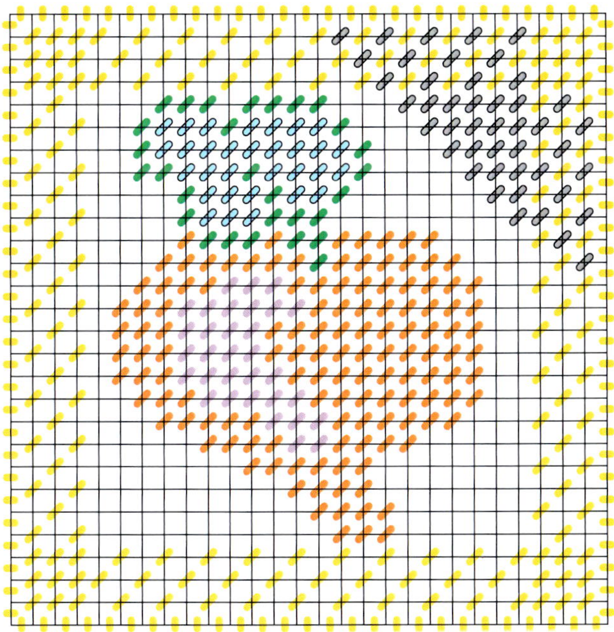

Green Pepper Coaster (28 x 28 threads)

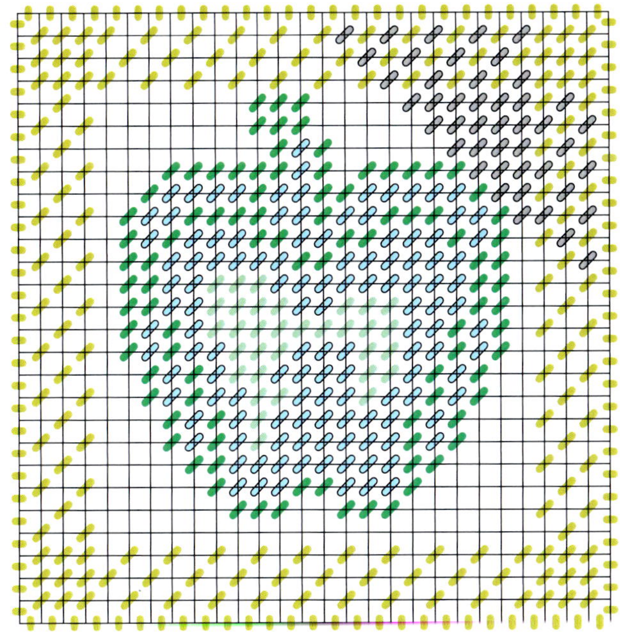

Mushroom Coaster (28 x 28 threads)

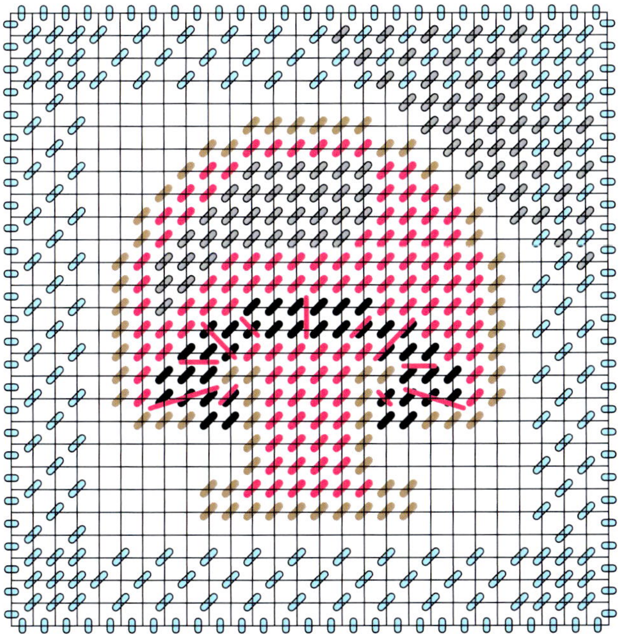

Pumpkin Coaster (28 x 28 threads)

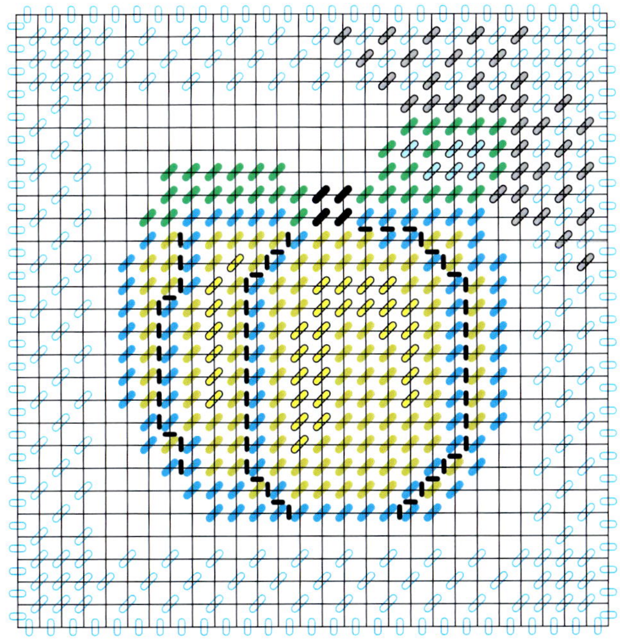

Blue Waves Tissue Box Cover

Size

$4^1/_2$"w x $5^3/_4$"h x $4^1/_2$"d
(fits a $4^1/_4$"w x $5^1/_4$"h x $4^1/_4$"d boutique tissue box)

Supplies

Two $10^1/_2$" x $13^1/_2$" sheets of 10 mesh plastic canvas
Medium weight yarn
#20 tapestry needle

Stitches Used

Bargello Stitch, Gobelin Stitch, and Overcast Stitch

Instructions

Follow charts to cut and stitch tissue box cover pieces. Use black Overcast Stitches to join Sides along long edges. Join Top to Sides.

Design by Conn Baker Gibney.

Top (45 x 45 threads)

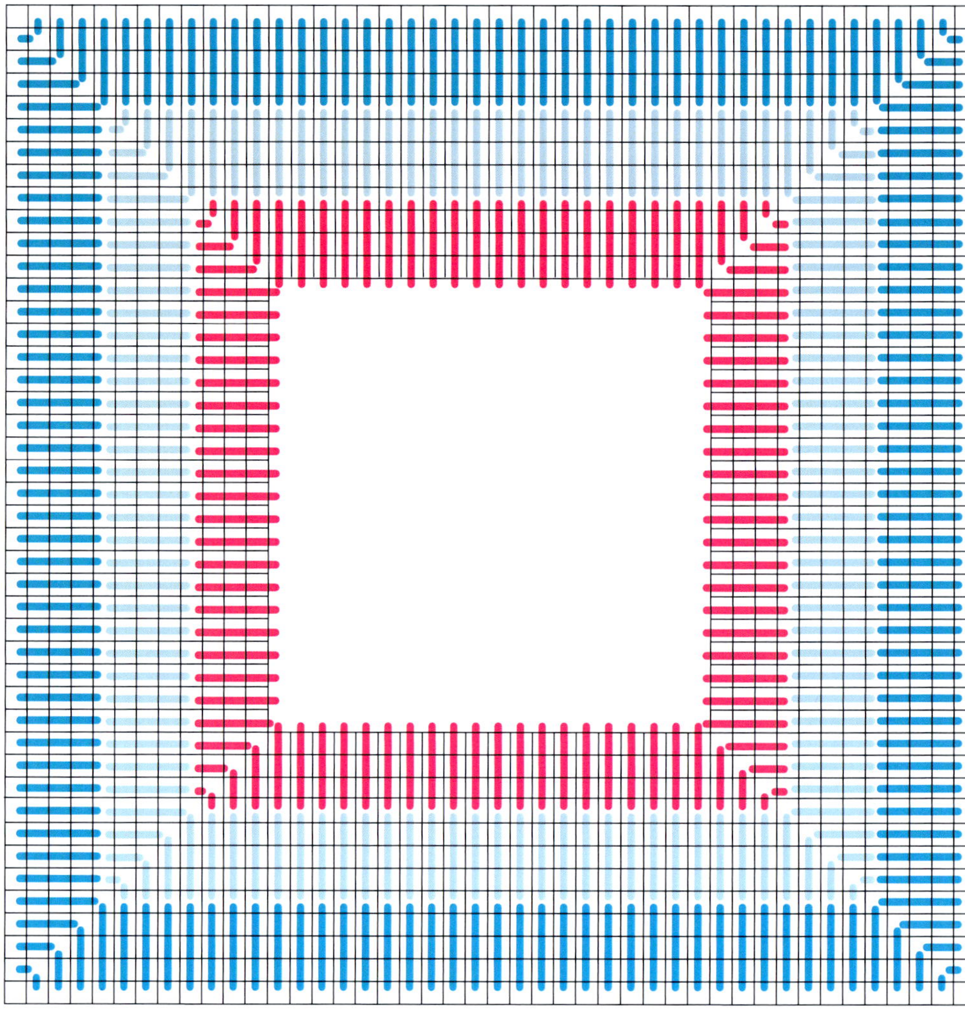

Color Key

- vy lt blue
- lt blue
- blue
- blue-grey
- royal
- dk blue
- black

Side (45 x 56 threads) (stitch 4)

Lightning Tissue Box Cover

Shown on page 24.

Size

$4^1/_2$"w x $5^1/_2$"h x $4^1/_2$"d
(fits a $4^1/_4$"w x $5^1/_4$"h x $4^1/_4$"d boutique tissue box)

Supplies

Two $10^1/_2$" x $13^1/_2$" sheets of 10 mesh plastic canvas
Medium weight yarn
#20 tapestry needle

Stitches Used

Bargello Stitch and Overcast Stitch

Instructions

Follow charts to cut and stitch tissue box cover pieces. Use vy lt blue Overcast Stitches to join Sides along long edges. Join Top to Sides.

Design by Conn Baker Gibney.

Top (46 x 46 threads)

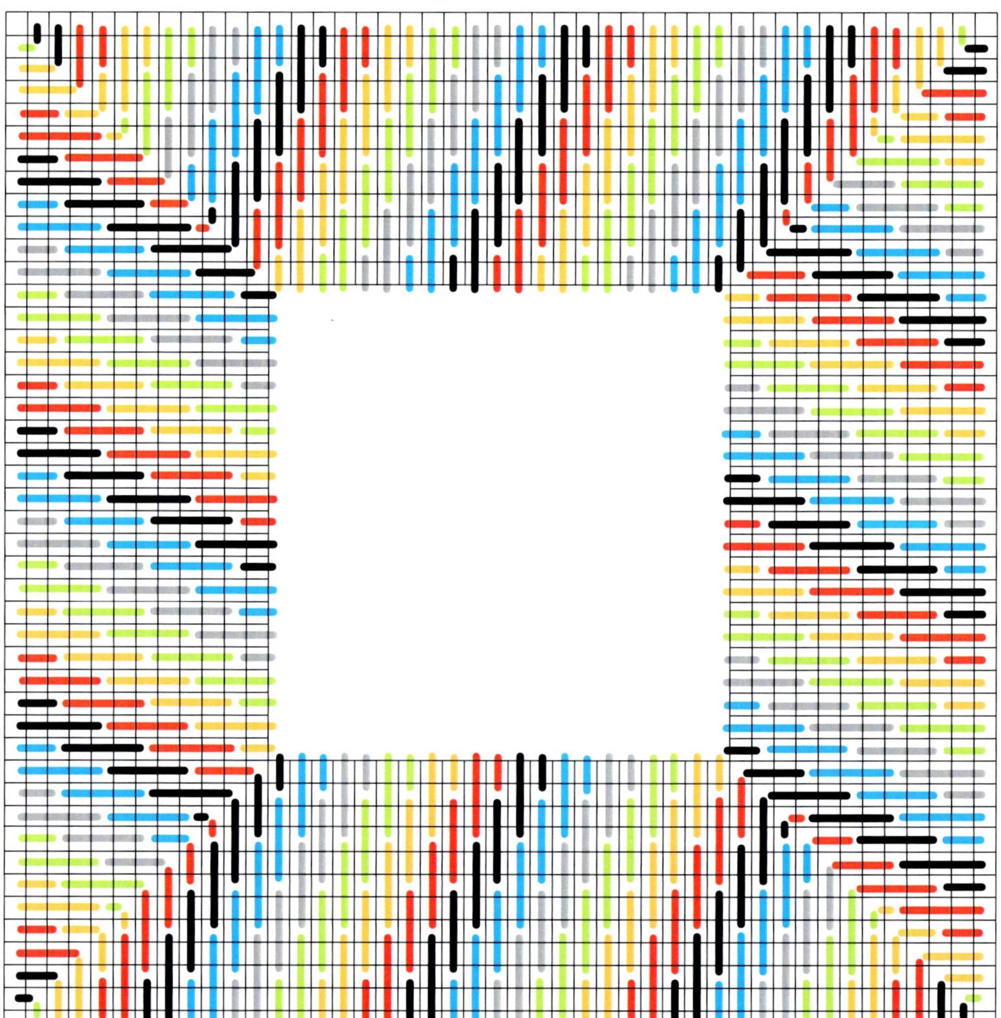

Color Key

- vy lt blue
- lt blue
- blue
- royal
- navy
- black

Side (46 x 55 threads) (stitch 4)

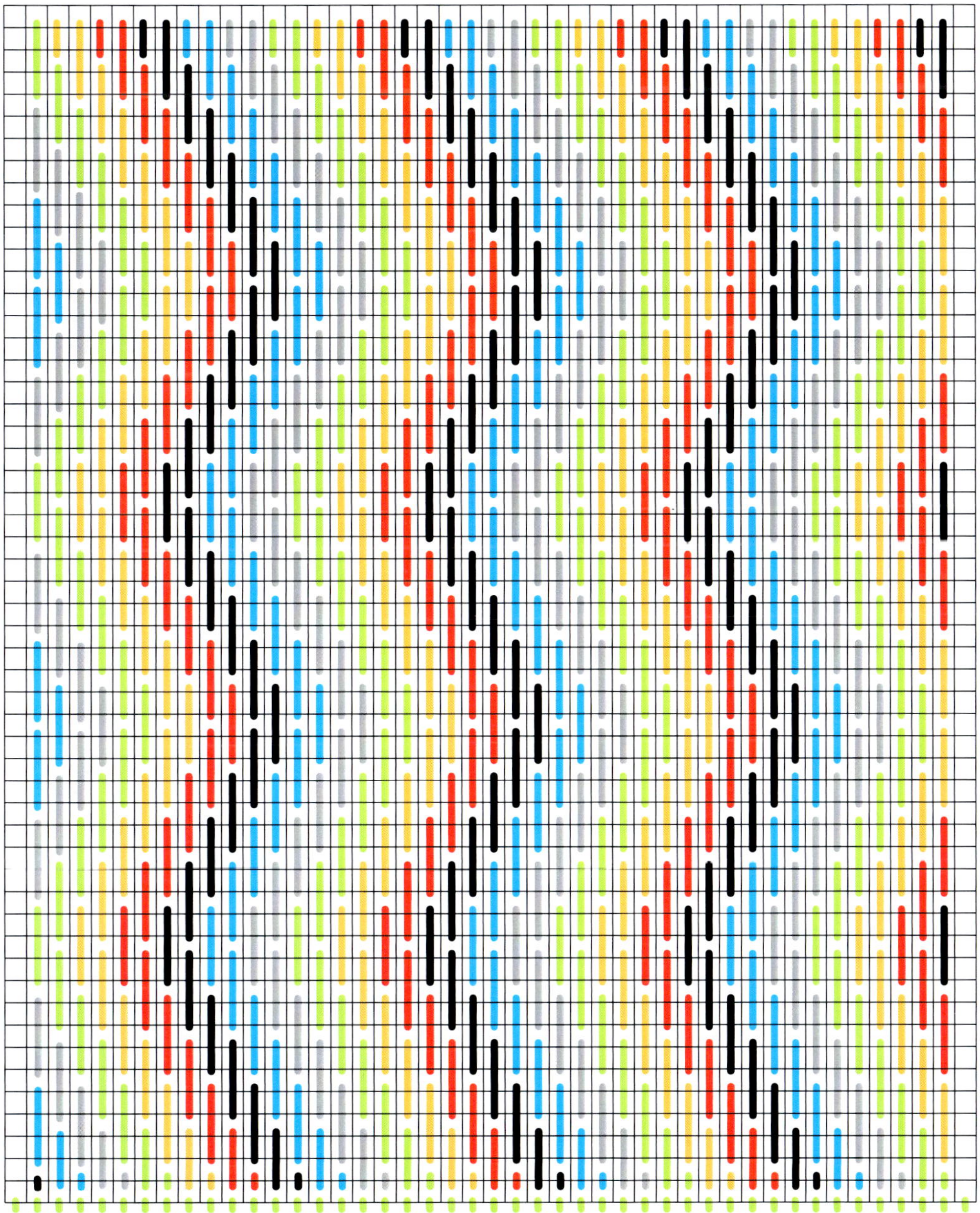

Tulips Tissue Box Cover

Shown on page 24.

Size

4½"w x 5½"h x 4½"d
(fits a 4¼"w x 5¼"h x 4¼"d boutique tissue box)

Supplies

Two 10½" x 13½" sheets of 10 mesh plastic canvas
Medium weight yarn
#20 tapestry needle

Stitches Used

Bargello Stitch and Overcast Stitch

Instructions

Follow charts to cut and stitch tissue box cover pieces. Use black Overcast Stitches to join Sides along long edges. Join Top to Sides.

Design by Conn Baker Gibney.

Top (46 x 46 threads)

Side (46 x 56 threads) (stitch 4)

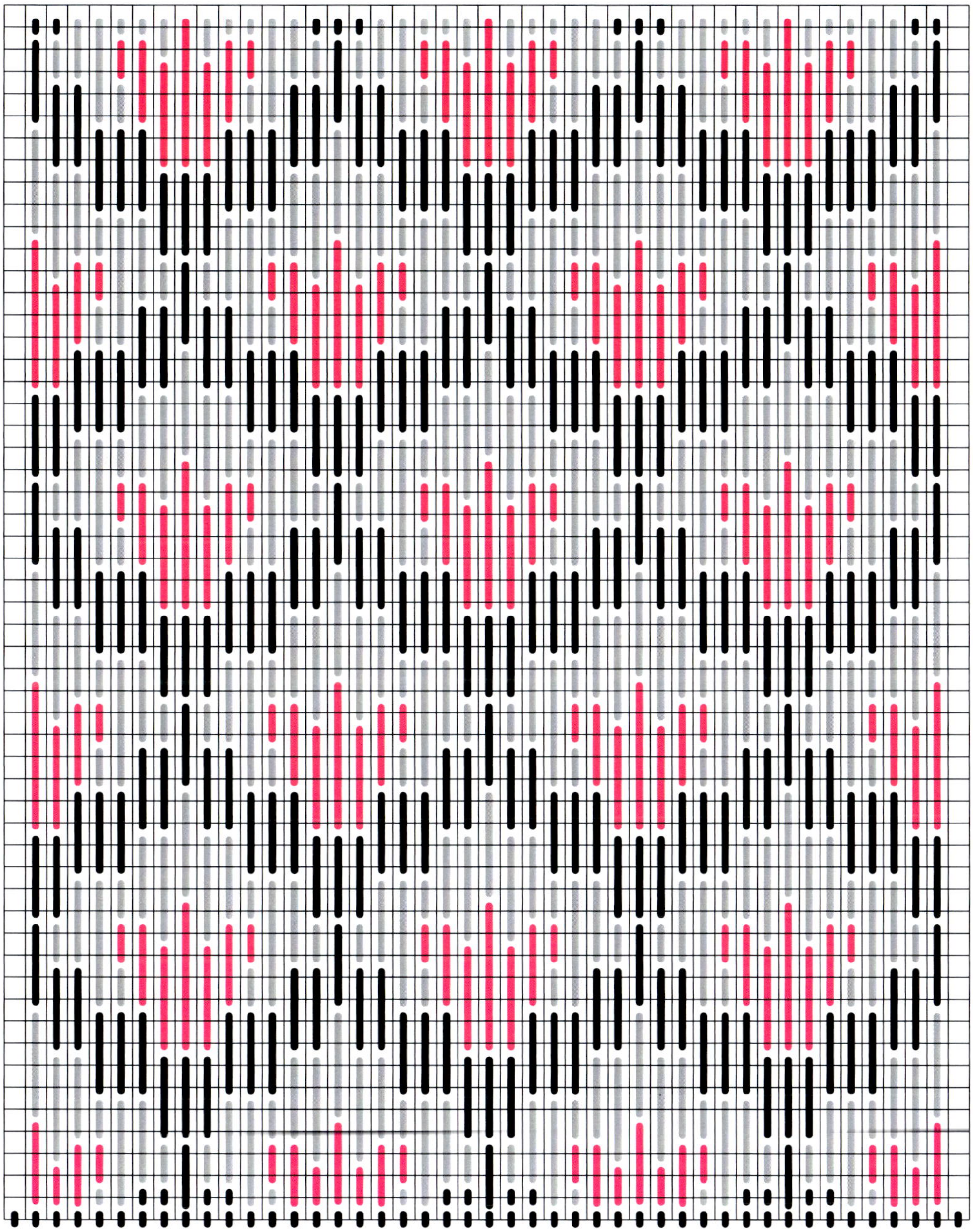

Quilt-Block Coasters

Size

4"w x 4"h each

Supplies

One 10 1/2" x 13 1/2" sheet of 7 mesh plastic canvas
Medium weight yarn
#16 tapestry needle
Cork or felt and craft glue (optional)

Stitches Used

Diagonal Mosaic Stitch, Gobelin Stitch, Overcast Stitch, Scotch Stitch, and Tent Stitch

Instructions

Follow chart to cut and stitch desired Coaster. If backing is desired, cut cork or felt slightly smaller than Coaster; glue to wrong side of Coaster.

Designs by James R. Green.

Color Key

- ecru
- blue
- dk blue

Coaster #1 (26 x 26 threads)

Coaster #2 (26 x 26 threads)

Coaster #3 (26 x 26 threads)

Coaster #4 (26 x 26 threads)

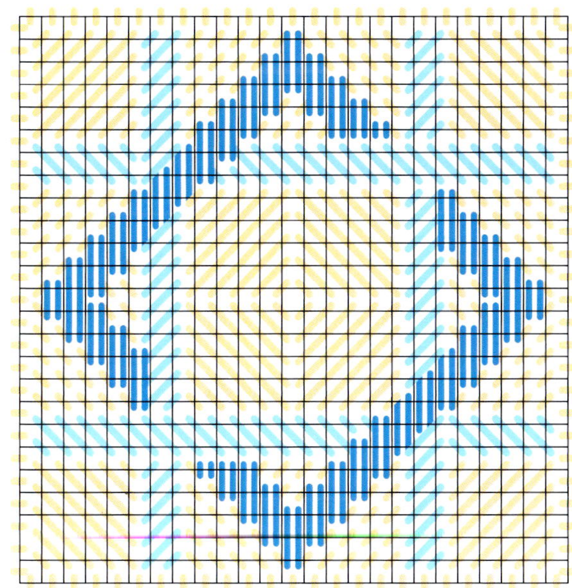

Coaster #5 (26 x 26 threads)

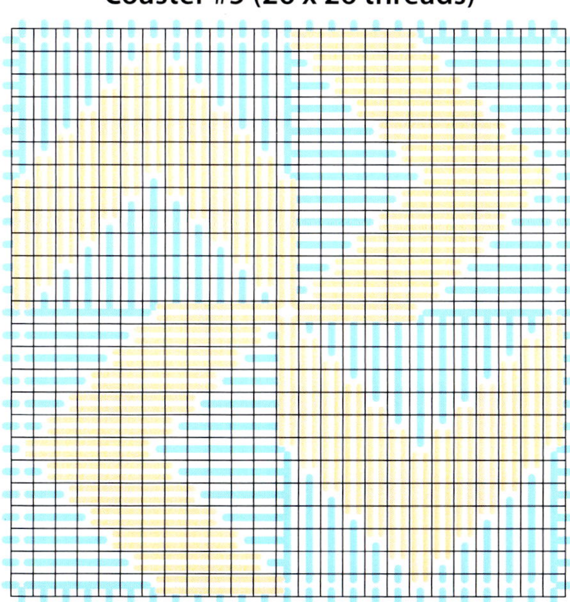

Coaster #6 (26 x 26 threads)

Approx. Size

4 1/4"w x 4 1/4"h each

Supplies for each Coaster

One 10 1/2" x 13 1/2" sheet of 7 mesh plastic canvas
Medium weight yarn
#16 tapestry needle
Cork or felt and craft glue (optional)

Stitches Used

Backstitch, Gobelin Stitch, Overcast Stitch, and Tent Stitch

Instructions

Follow chart to cut and stitch desired Coaster, completing background as indicated on chart. If backing is desired, cut cork or felt slightly smaller than Coaster. Glue cork or felt to back of Coaster.

Hobby Coasters

Color Key

- white
- yellow
- orange
- red
- purple
- blue
- green
- tan
- grey
- black

Sewing Thread (31 x 31 threads)

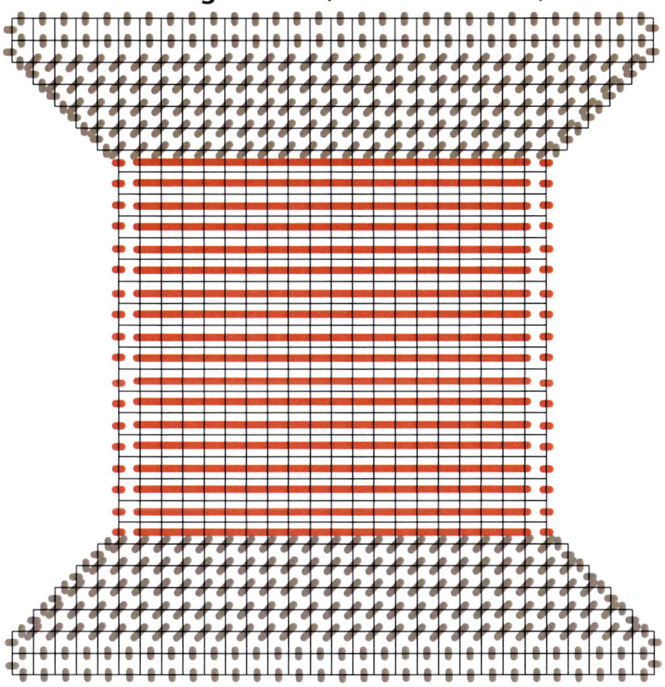

Artist Palette (30 x 30 threads)

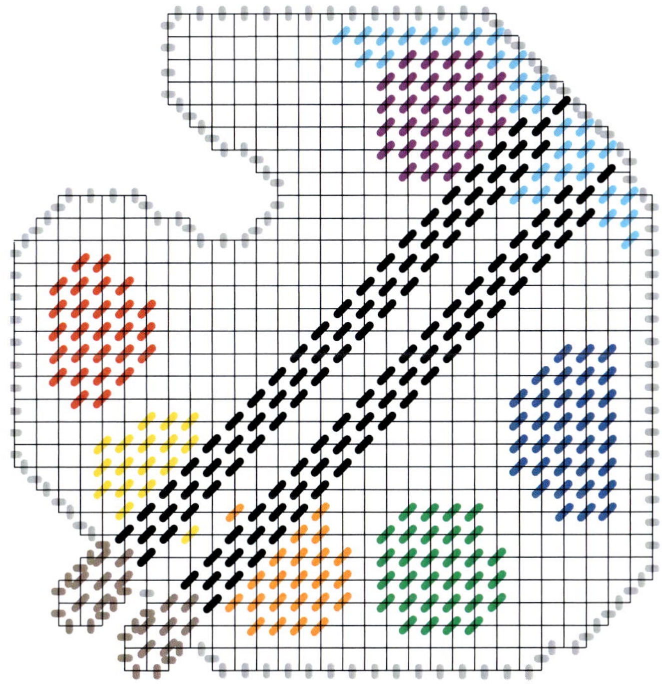

Bridge (27 x 27 threads)

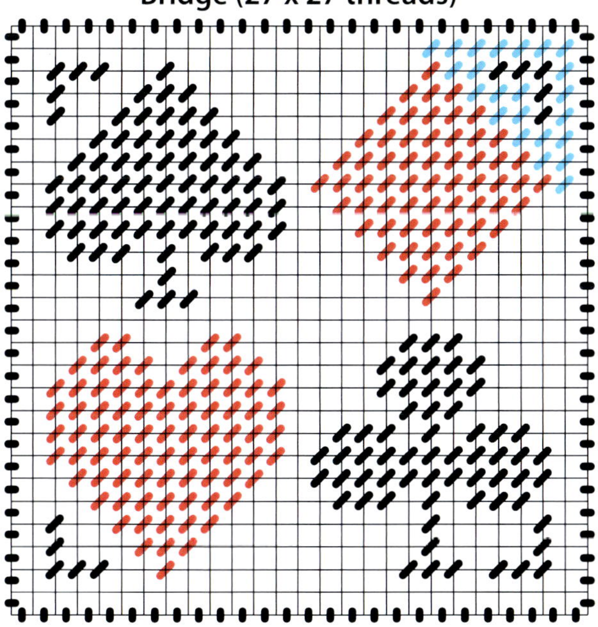

Piano (27 x 30 threads)

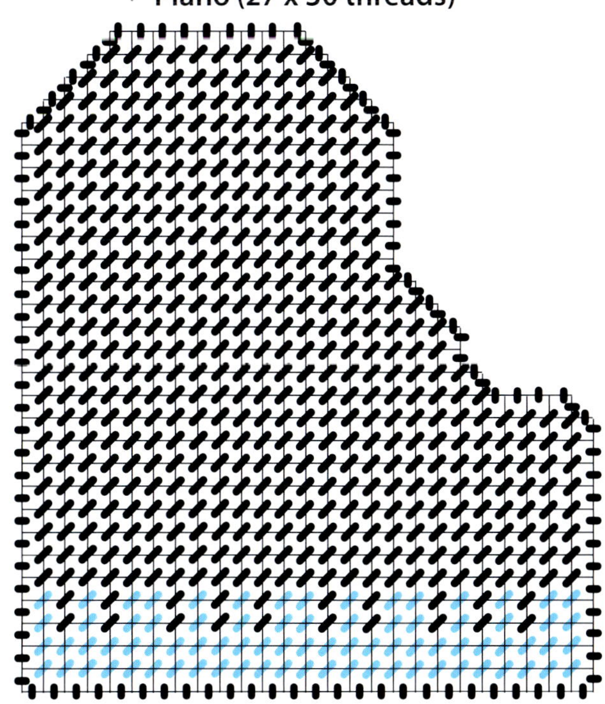

Sewing Thread design by Teresa E. Barnett.
Artist Palette design by Cheryl Krepps.
Bridge design by James R. Green.
Piano design by Michele Sartain.

Big Beak Birds

Approximate Size

4 3/8"w x 2"h x 3 1/4"d each

Supplies

10½" x 13½" sheets of 7 mesh plastic canvas
Medium weight yarn
#16 tapestry needle
Craft glue
For American Goldfinch: Two 12mm oval wiggle eyes
For Blue Jay: Two 12mm oval wiggle eyes
For Cardinal: Two 12mm oval wiggle eyes
For Eastern Bluebird: Two 15mm oval wiggle eyes
For Hummingbird: Two 12mm oval wiggle eyes
For Owl: Two 9mm yellow cat eyes or wiggle eyes
For Pileated Woodpecker: Two 12mm oval wiggle eyes
For Red-winged Blackbird: Two 15mm oval wiggle eyes

Instructions

American Goldfinch

Follow charts to cut and stitch American Goldfinch pieces. Refer to photo for yarn colors used to join pieces. With wrong sides together, match ◒'s to join Top to Back along unworked threads of Top. Match ▲'s to join Bottom to Back along unworked threads. Glue eyes to Top.

Blue Jay

Follow charts to cut and stitch Blue Jay pieces. Refer to photo for yarn colors used to join pieces. Match ★'s to join unworked edges of crest. With wrong sides together, match ◒'s to join Top to Back along unworked threads of Top. Match ▲'s to join Bottom to Back along unworked threads. Glue eyes to Top.

Cardinal

Follow charts to cut and stitch Cardinal pieces. Refer to photo for yarn colors used to join pieces. Match ★'s to join unworked edges of crest. With wrong sides together, match ◒'s to join Top to Back along unworked threads of Top. Match ▲'s to join Bottom to Back along unworked threads. Glue eyes to Top.

Eastern Bluebird

Follow charts to cut and stitch Eastern Bluebird pieces. Refer to photo for yarn colors used to join pieces. With wrong sides together, match ◒'s to join Top to Back along unworked threads of Top. Match ▲'s to join Bottom to Back along unworked threads. Glue eyes to Top.

Hummingbird

Follow charts to cut and stitch Hummingbird pieces. Refer to photo for yarn colors used to join pieces. With wrong sides together, match ◒'s to join Top to Back along unworked threads of Top. Match ▲'s to join Bottom to Back along unworked threads. Glue eyes to Top.

Owl

Follow charts and to cut and stitch Owl pieces. Refer to photo for yarn colors used to join pieces. With wrong sides together, match ◒'s to join Top to Back along unworked threads of Top. Match ▲'s to join Bottom to Back along unworked threads. Glue eyes to Top. Trim Fringe to 3/8" and separate into plies.

Pileated Woodpecker

Follow charts to cut and stitch Pileated Woodpecker pieces. Refer to photo for yarn colors used to join pieces. Match ★'s to join unworked edges of crest. With wrong sides together, match ◒'s to join Top to Back along unworked threads of Top. Match ▲'s to join Bottom to Back along unworked threads. Glue eyes to Top.

Red-winged Blackbird

Follow charts to cut and stitch Red-winged Blackbird pieces. Refer to photo for yarn colors used to join pieces. With wrong sides together, match ◒'s to join Top to Back along unworked threads of Top. Match ▲'s to join Bottom to Back along unworked threads. Glue eyes to Top.

Designs by Sheri Allsop Krohn.

HUMMINGBIRD

Color Key

- white
- ecru
- red
- olive
- lt grey
- dk grey

Top (13 x 13 threads)

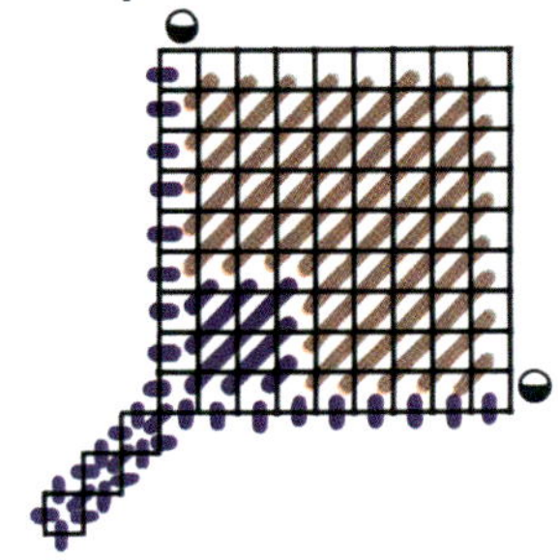

Back (21 x 21 threads)

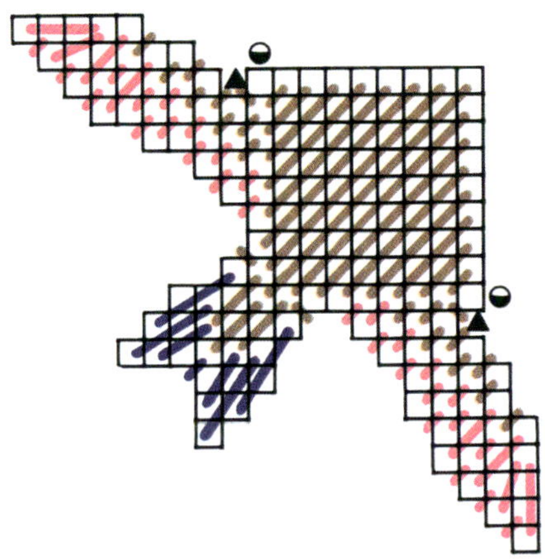

Bottom (21 x 21 threads)

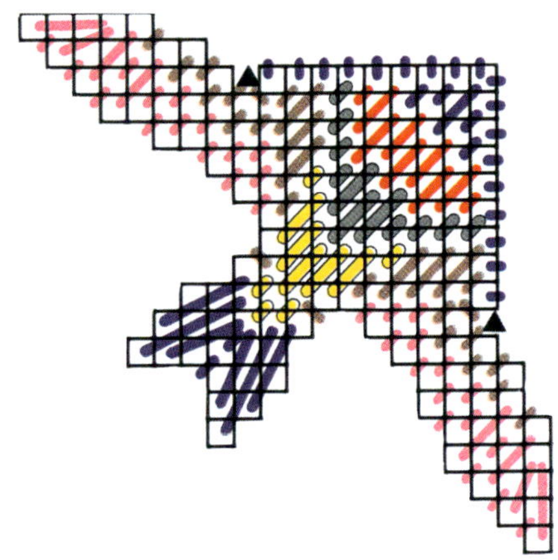

BLUE JAY

Color Key

- white
- ecru
- blue
- dk grey
- black
- black 1-ply

Top (17 x 17 threads)

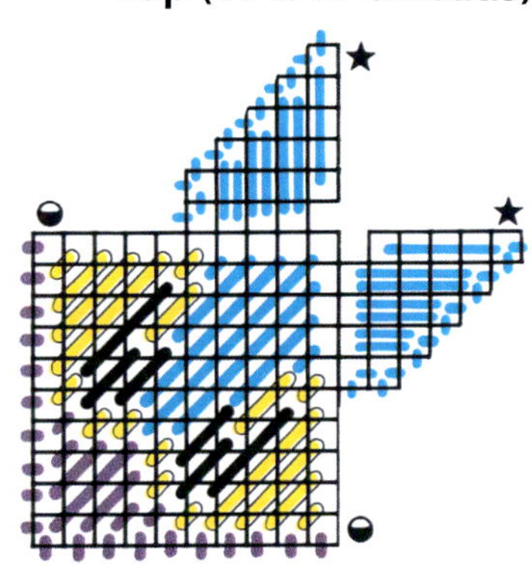

Back (21 x 21 threads)

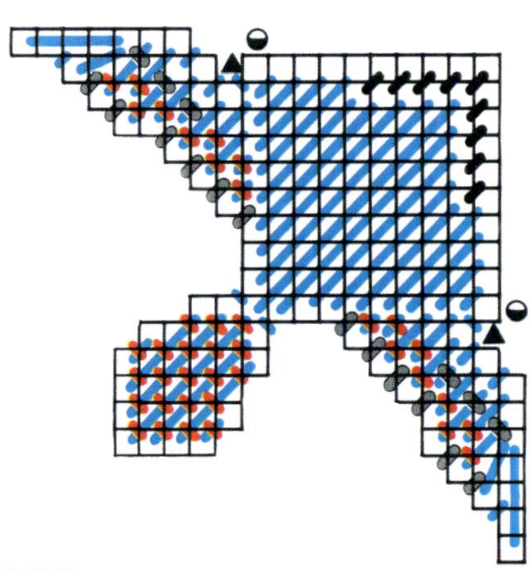

Bottom (21 x 21 threads)

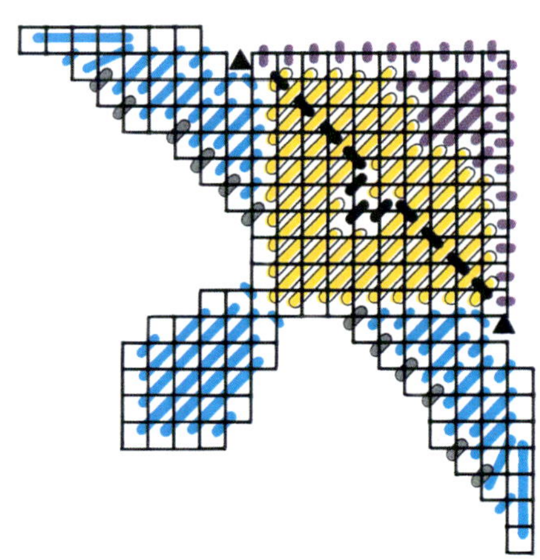

PILEATED WOODPECKER

Color Key
- white
- red
- dk grey
- black

Top (17 x 17 threads)

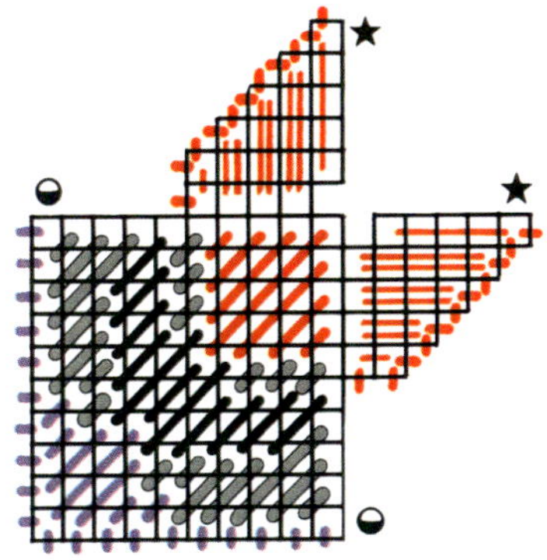

Back (21 x 21 threads)

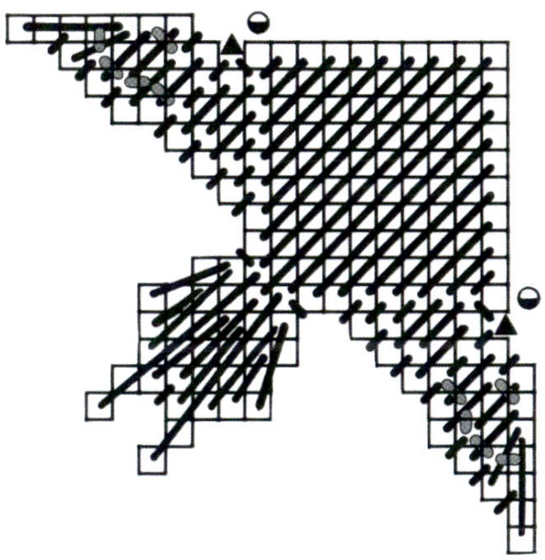

Bottom (21 x 21 threads)

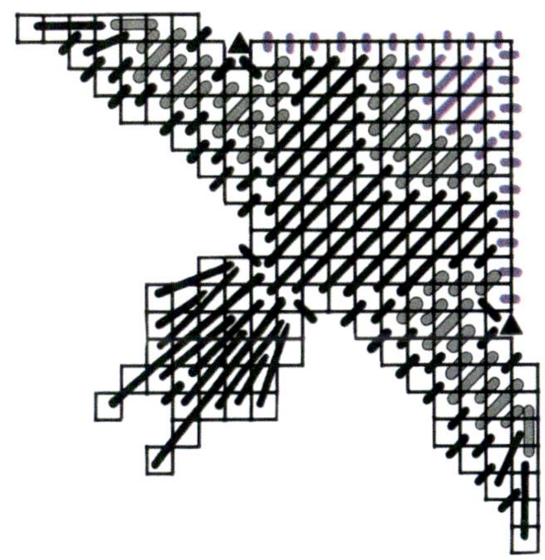

RED-WINGED BLACKBIRD

Color Key
- yellow
- red
- dk grey
- black

Top (11 x 11 threads)

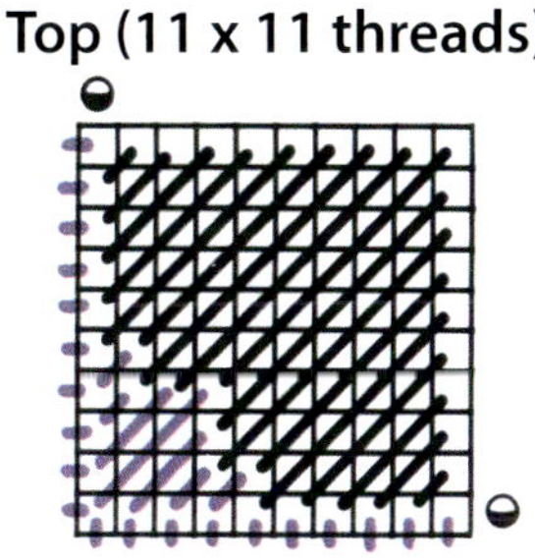

Back (21 x 21 threads)

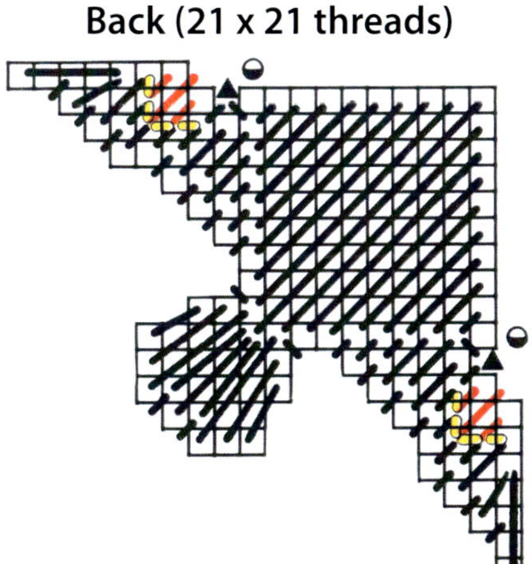

Bottom (21 x 21 threads)

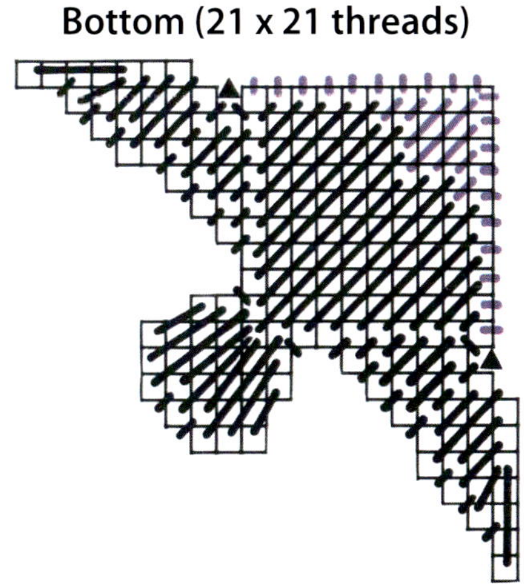

CARDINAL

Color Key
- orange
- red
- black

Top (17 x 17 threads)

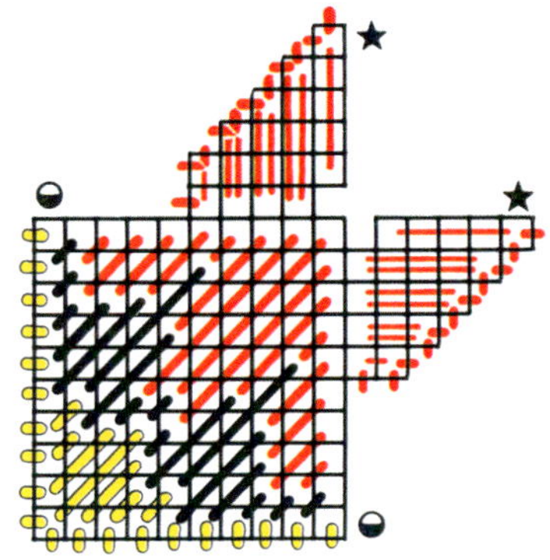

Back (21 x 21 threads)

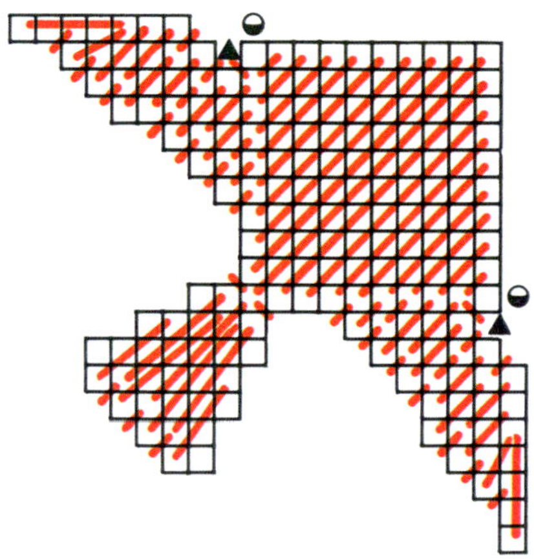

Bottom (21 x 21 threads)

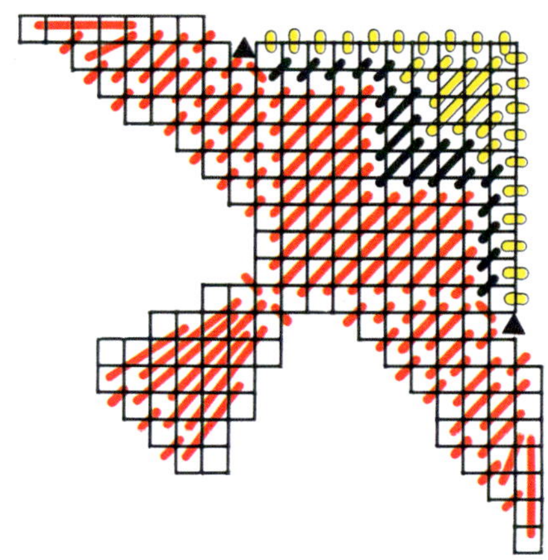

EASTERN BLUEBIRD

Color Key
- white
- peach
- blue
- dk grey

Top (11 x 11 threads)

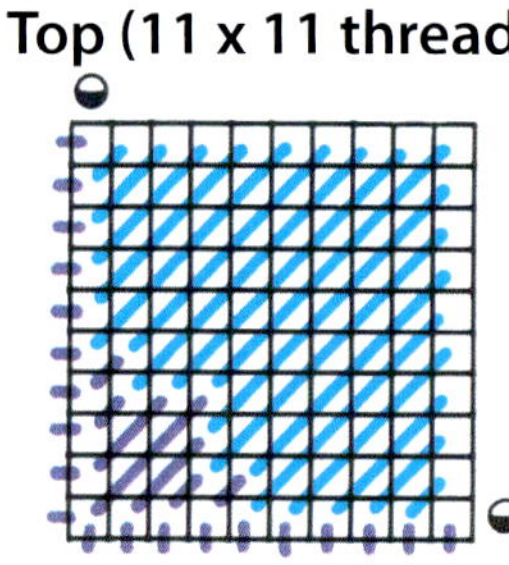

Back (21 x 21 threads)

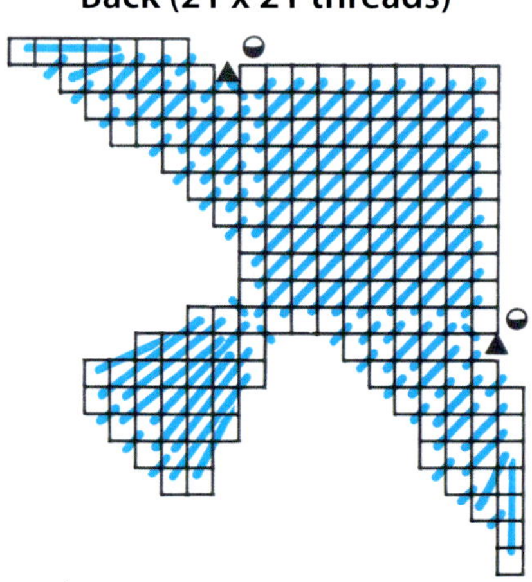

Bottom (21 x 21 threads)

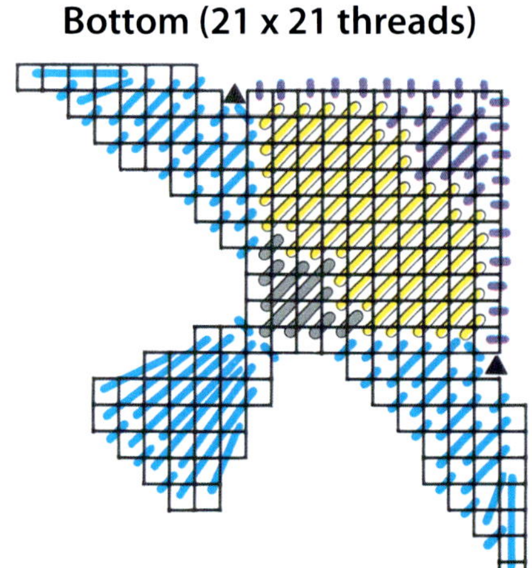

OWL

Color Key

- ecru
- brown
- black
- ecru Fringe Stitch
- brown Fringe Stitch

Top (13 x 13 threads)

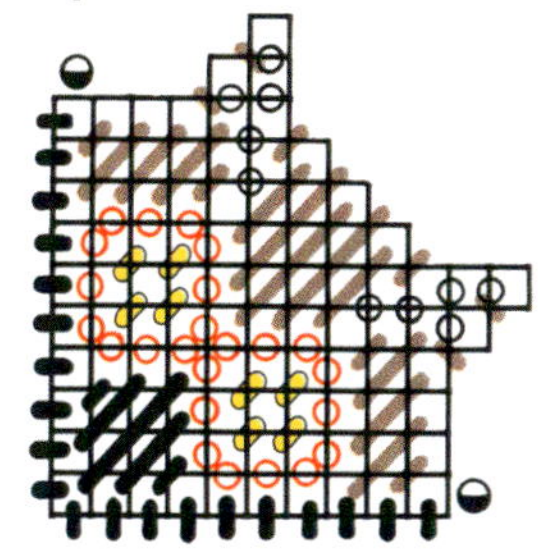

Back (22 x 22 threads)

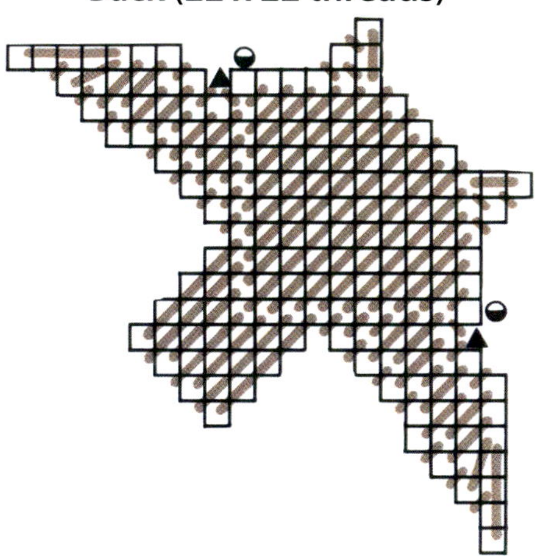

Bottom (21 x 21 threads)

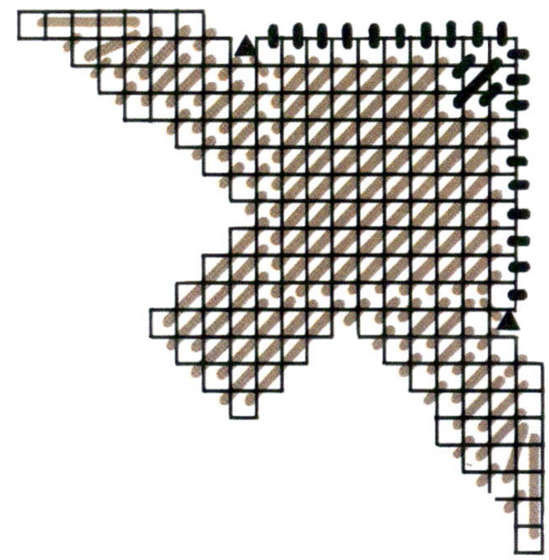

AMERICAN GOLDFINCH

Color Key

- white
- yellow
- lt grey
- black

Top (11 x 11 threads)

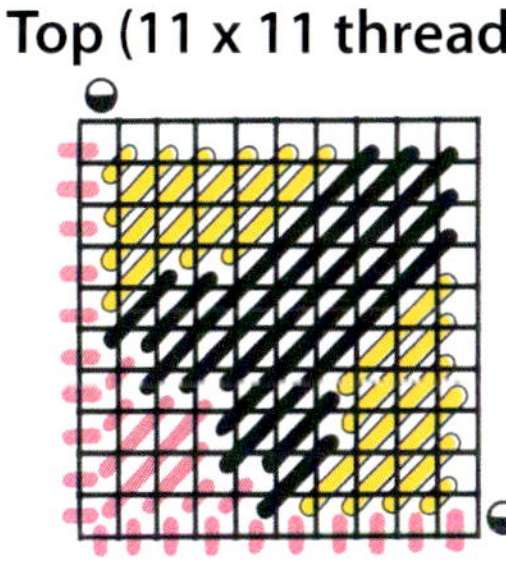

Back (21 x 21 threads)

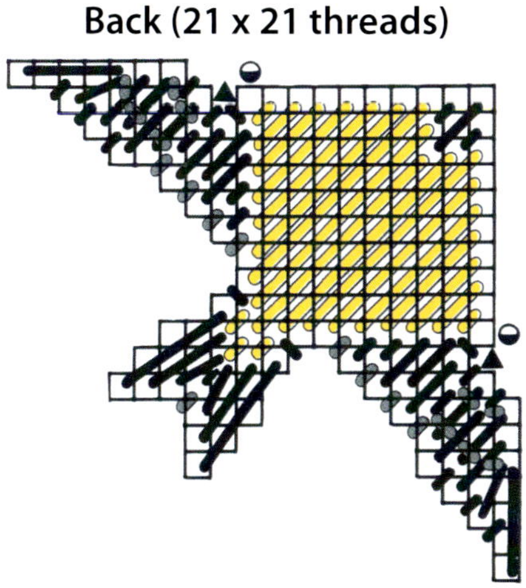

Bottom (21 x 21 threads)

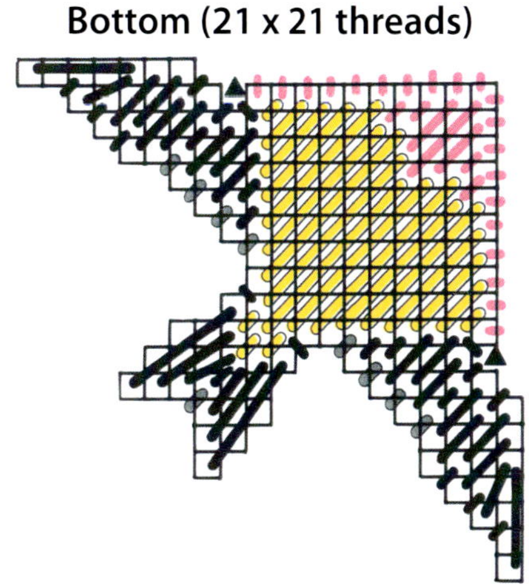

"Sea-sonal" Fun

Size

4"w x 4"h

Supplies

One 10 1/2" x 13 1/2" sheet of 7 mesh plastic canvas
Medium weight yarn
#16 tapestry needle
Cork or felt and craft glue (optional)

Stitches Used

Gobelin Stitch, Overcast Stitch, and Tent Stitch

Instructions

Follow chart to cut and stitch Coaster. If backing is desired, cut cork or felt slightly smaller than Coaster. Glue cork or felt to back.

Design by Terry A. Ricioli.

Color Key

- white
- yellow
- blue
- black

Coaster (29 x 29 threads)

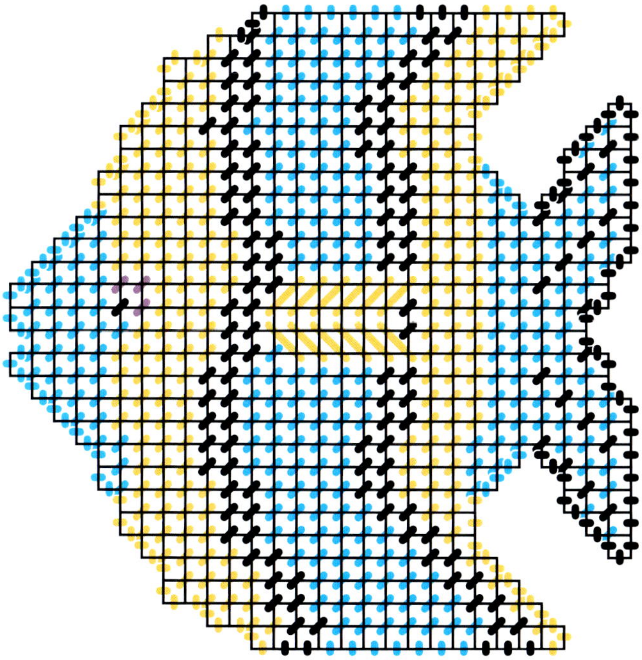

Pinwheels Tissue Box Cover

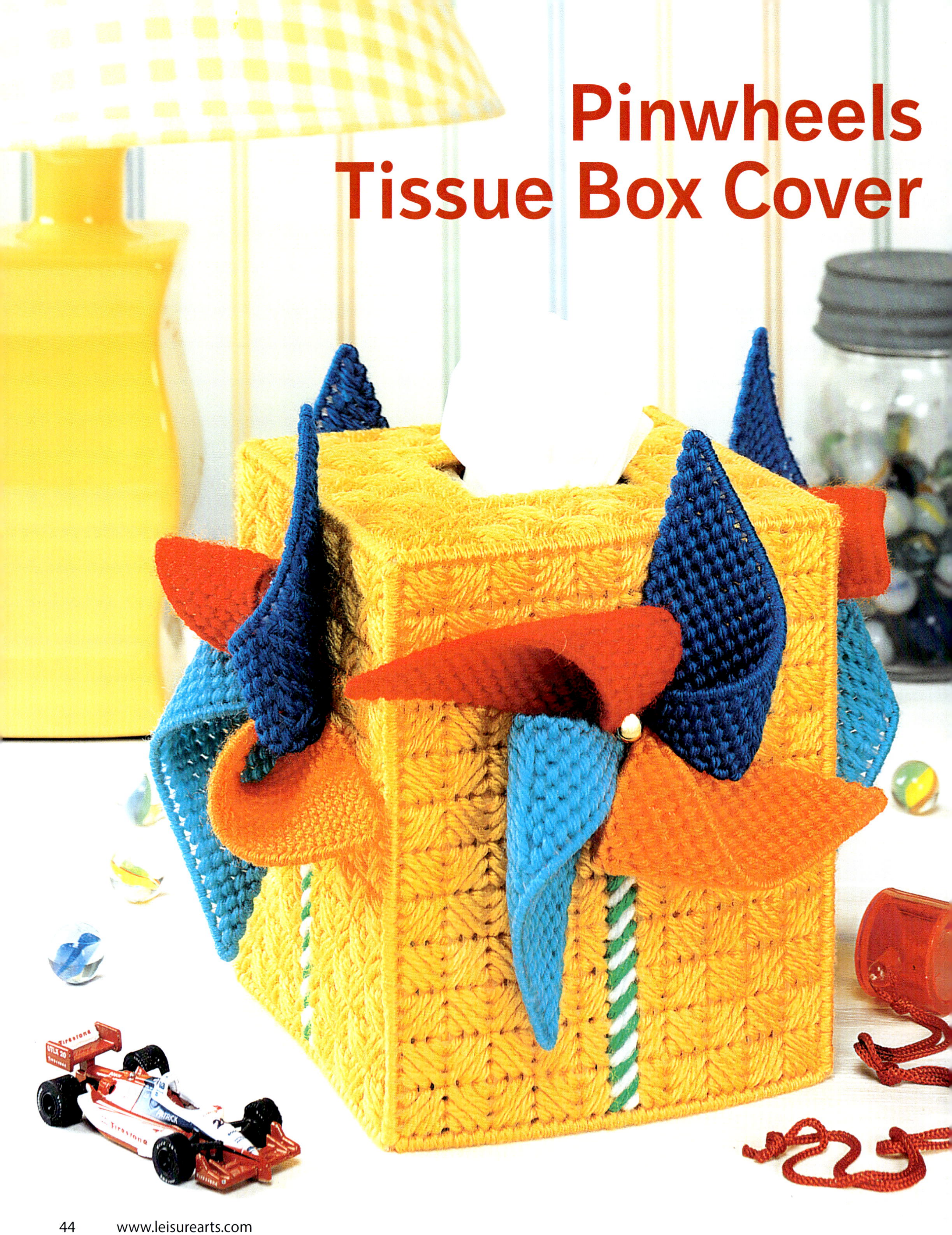

Size

$4^1/_2$"w x $5^1/_2$"h x $4^1/_2$"d
(fits a $4^1/_4$"w x $5^1/_4$"h x $4^1/_4$"d boutique tissue box)

Supplies

Three $10^1/_2$" x $13^1/_2$" sheets of 7 mesh plastic canvas
Medium weight yarn
Four $^3/_4$" paper fasteners
#16 tapestry needle

Stitches Used

Alternating Scotch Stitch, Gobelin Stitch, Overcast Stitch, and Tent Stitch

Instructions

Follow charts and photos to cut and stitch tissue box cover pieces, leaving grey shaded areas unworked. Use matching color Overcast Stitches for all joining. Matching long edges, join Sides. Join Top to Sides.

For each Pinwheel, turn Pinwheel piece over. Work stitches in grey shaded areas on wrong side of Pinwheel. With right side up, fold corners of Pinwheel indicated by arrows to center and tack. Insert paper fastener in Pinwheel and Side at ♥. Secure fastener on inside of tissue box cover.

Design by Conn Baker Gibney.

Pastel Color Key	Bright Color Key
white	white
lt yellow	yellow
lt pink	orange
lt purple	red
purple	green
lt blue	dk blue
lt green	turquoise

Pinwheel (30 x 30 threads) (stitch 4)

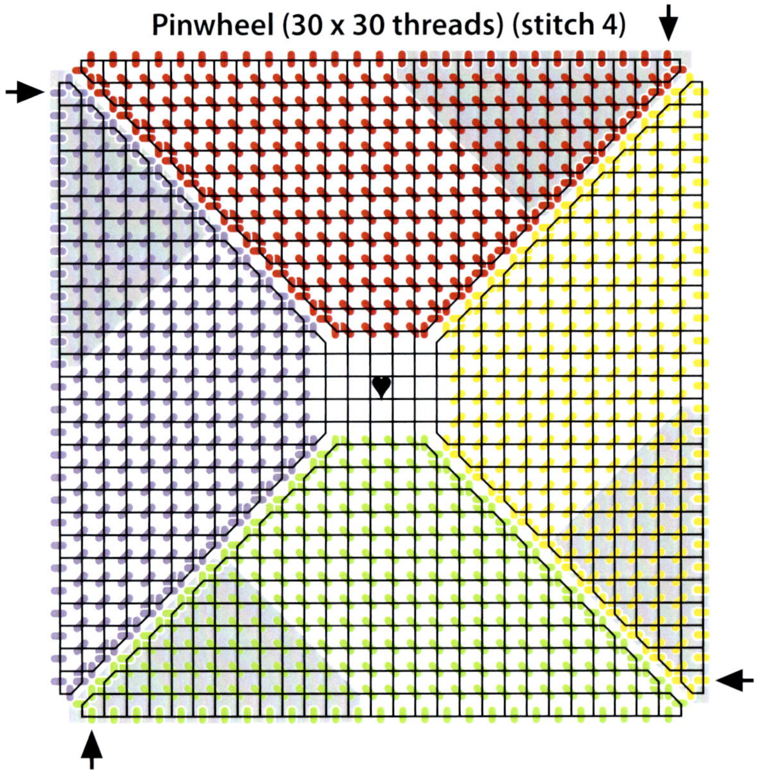

Side (32 x 38 threads) (stitch 4)

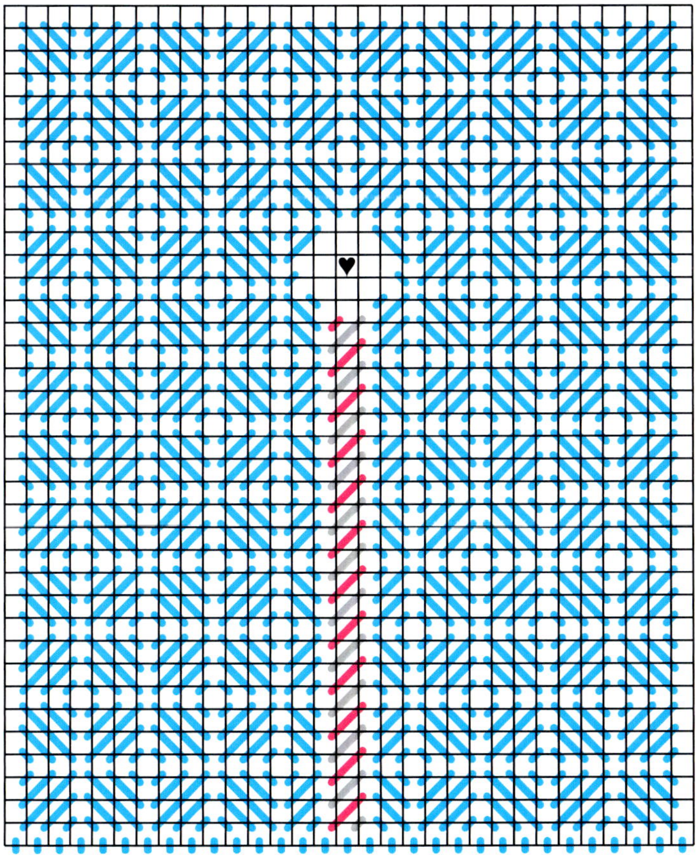

Top (32 x 32 threads)

A Year of Door Hangers

Size
$4\frac{7}{8}$"w x $10\frac{5}{8}$"h each

Supplies for each Door Hanger

one $10\frac{1}{2}$"x $13\frac{1}{2}$" sheet of 7 mesh plastic canvas
Medium weight yam
#16 tapestry needle
March only: One 3" diameter plastic canvas circle
October only: Embroidery floss
December only: One 3" diameter plastic canvas circle

Stitches Used
Backstitch, Cross Stitch, French Knot, Fringe Stitch, Gobelin Stitch, Overcast Stitch, and Tent Stitch

Instructions
Follow charts to cut and stitch Door Hangers. Before working Backstitch or French Knots, complete background of Door Hanger with Tent Stitches as indicated on chart.

March
1. For Cart Wheel, cut away 2 threads from outer edge of 3" diameter plastic canvas circle. Cut away 4 threads from inside of plastic canvas circle. Follow chart to stitch Cart Wheel.
2. Cut a 24" length of brown yarn. Secure yarn on wrong side of Cart Wheel by running yarn under the back of a few stitches. Refer to Cart Wheel Diagram to make spokes of Cart Wheel, working all stitches on wrong side. Run yarn across opening four times, securing yam on wrong side of Cart Wheel. after forming each spoke. To attach Cart Wheel to Door Hanger, center the intersection of spokes over the ▲ symbol on Door Hanger. Use brown to tack intersection of spokes to Door Hanger at ▲.

October
Refer to photo and use black to tack Tail to Door Hanger.

December
1. Refer to chart to cut Arms from 3" diameter plastic canvas circle. Follow chart to stitch Arms.
2. Refer to photo for placement and use white to tack Arms to Door Hanger. Use brown to tack Broom to Door Hanger.

Designs by Joan E. Ray.

JULY
HAPPY EASTER
FALL
DECEMBER
NOEL!

JANUARY

Color Key

- black
- red
- lt red
- dk red
- orange
- lt brown
- brown
- lt green
- green
- white
- red Fr. Knot

January (33 x 71 threads)

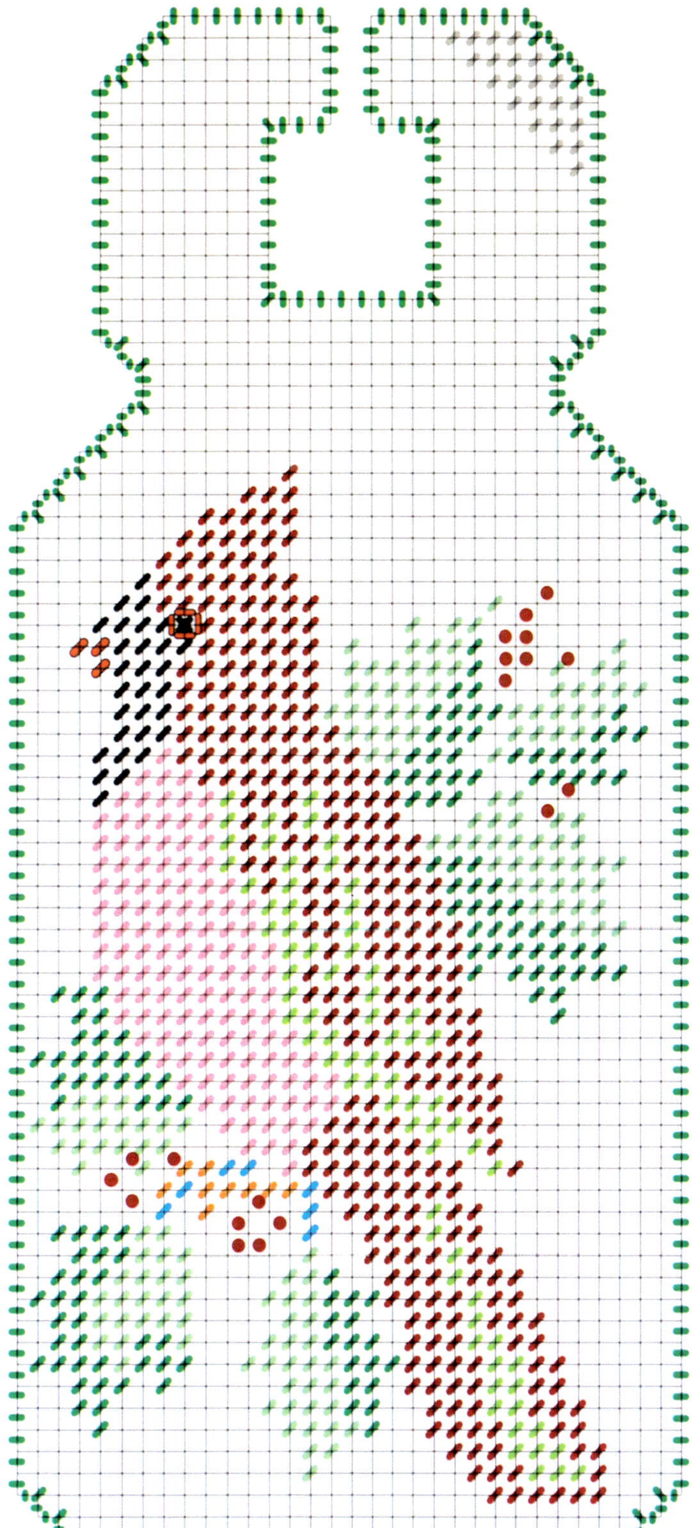

FEBRUARY

Color Key

- black
- red
- white

February (33 x 71 threads)

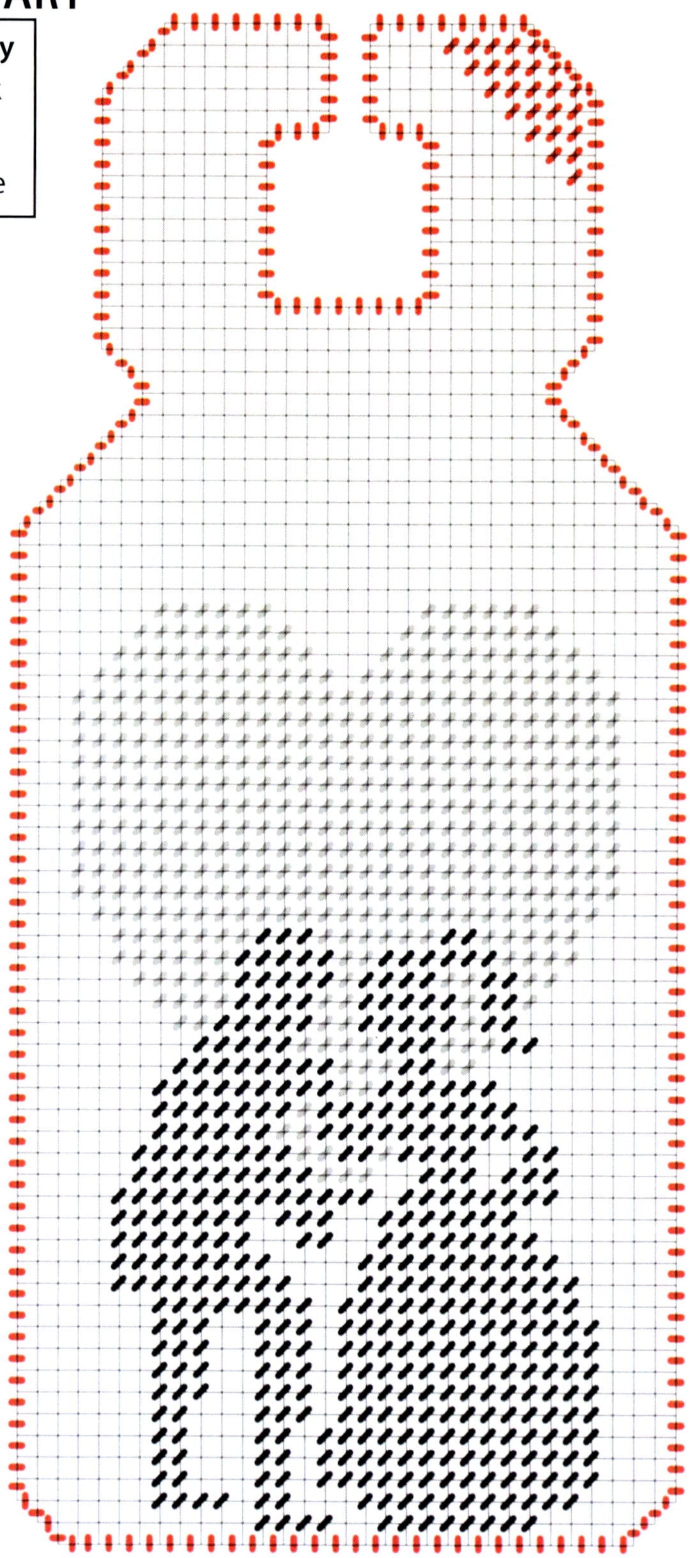

MARCH

Color Key

- lt pink
- lt orange
- orange
- blue
- dk brown
- tan
- yellow
- brown
- white
- lavender
- purple
- green
- pink

March Cart Wheel

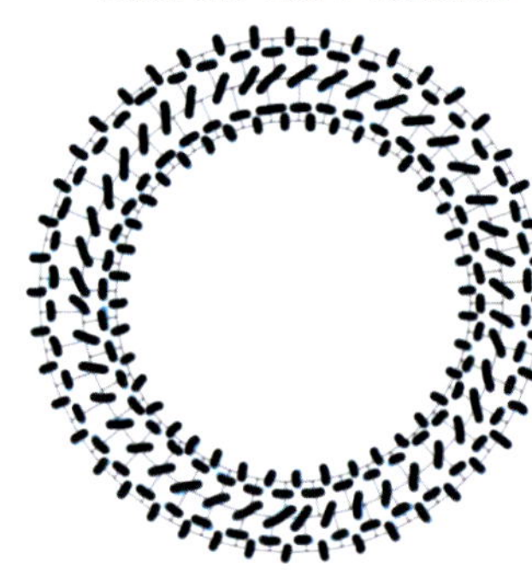

Cart Wheel Diagram

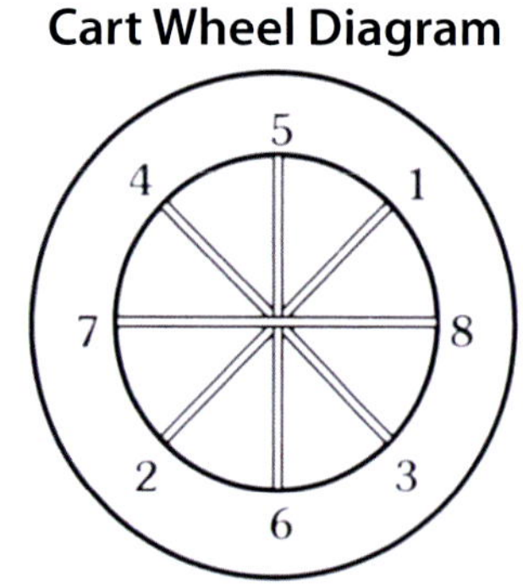

*(**Note:** Wrong side is shown.)*

March (33 x 71 threads)

April (33 x 71 threads)

APRIL

Color Key

orange	lavender
lt green	purple
green	pink
blue	yellow
white	

May (33 x 71 threads)

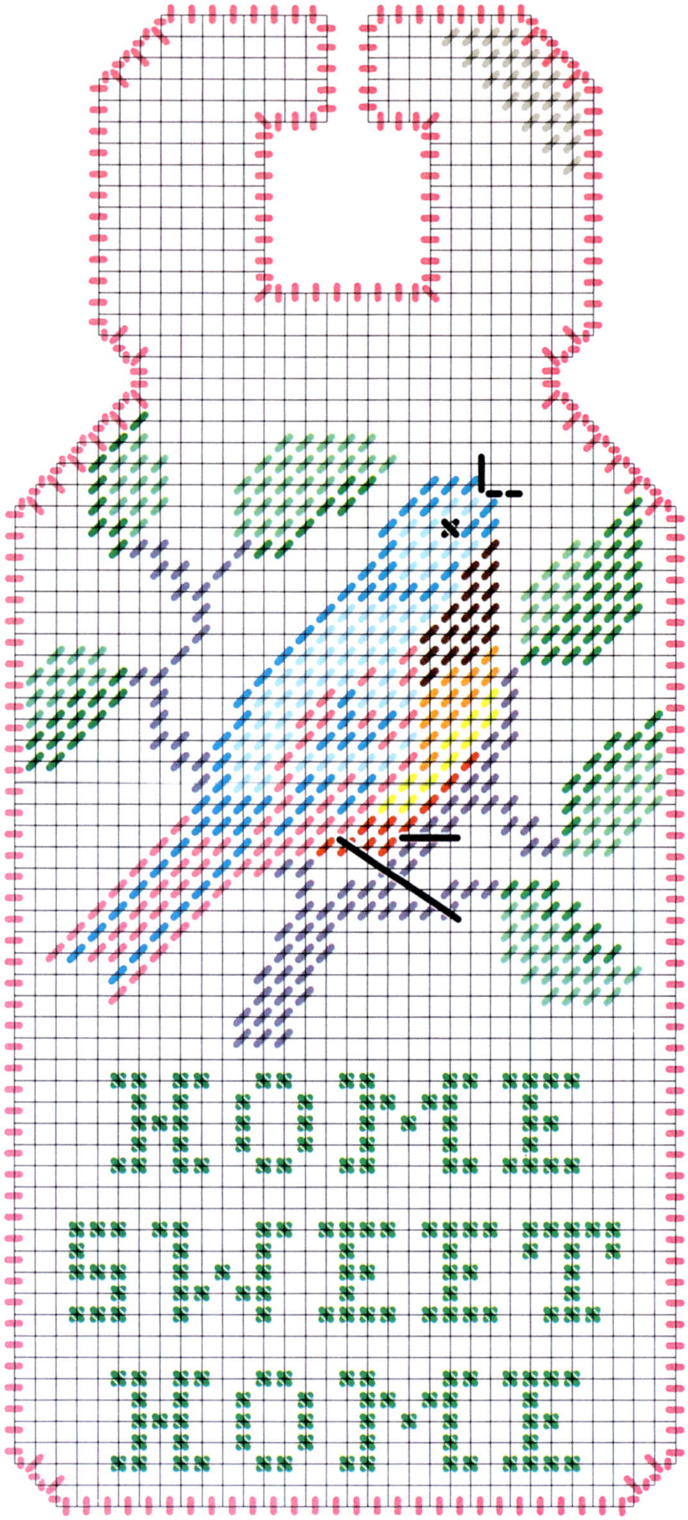

June (33 x 71 threads)

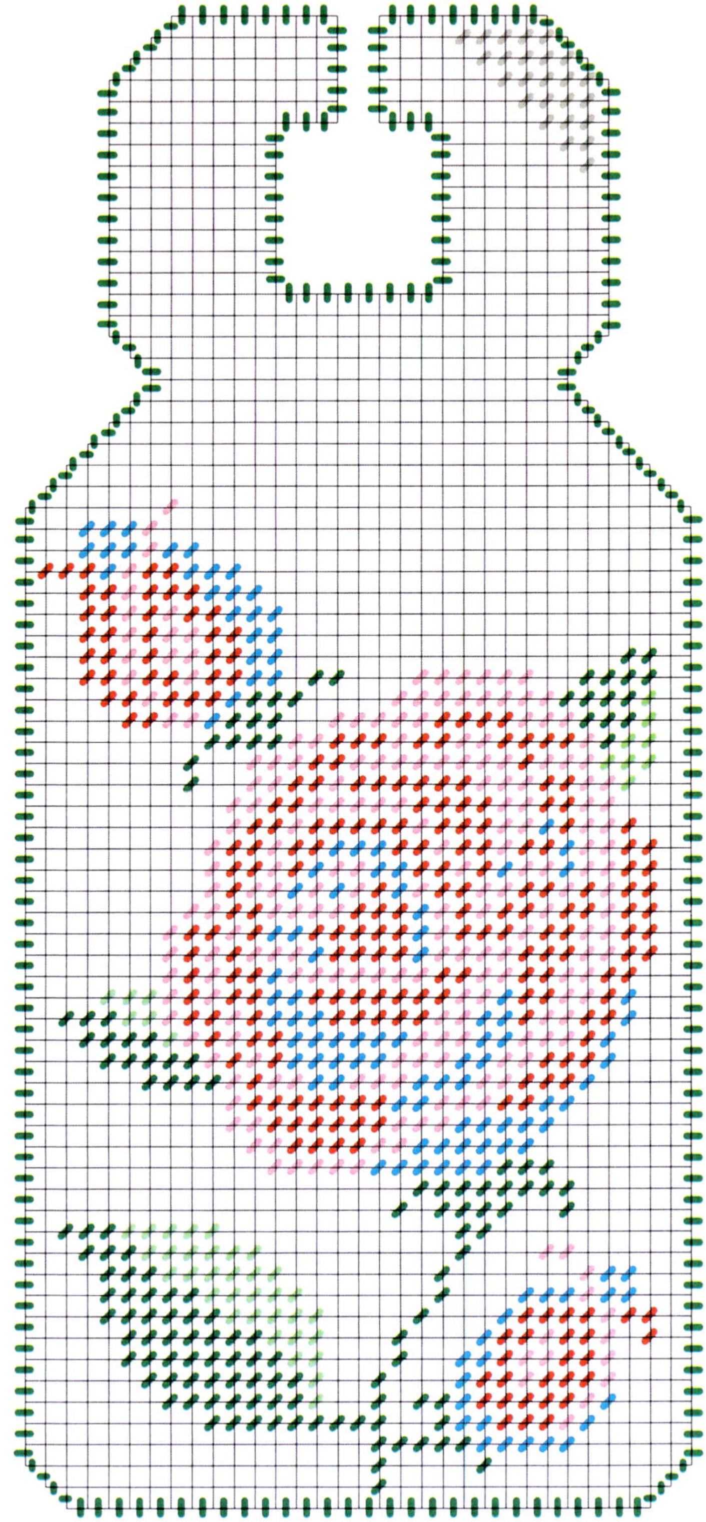

MAY

Color Key

black	ecru
dk peach	white
brown	dk blue
beige	green
blue	lt green
lt blue	peach

JUNE

Color Key

dk pink	lt green
pink	white
lt pink	green

July (33 x 71 threads)

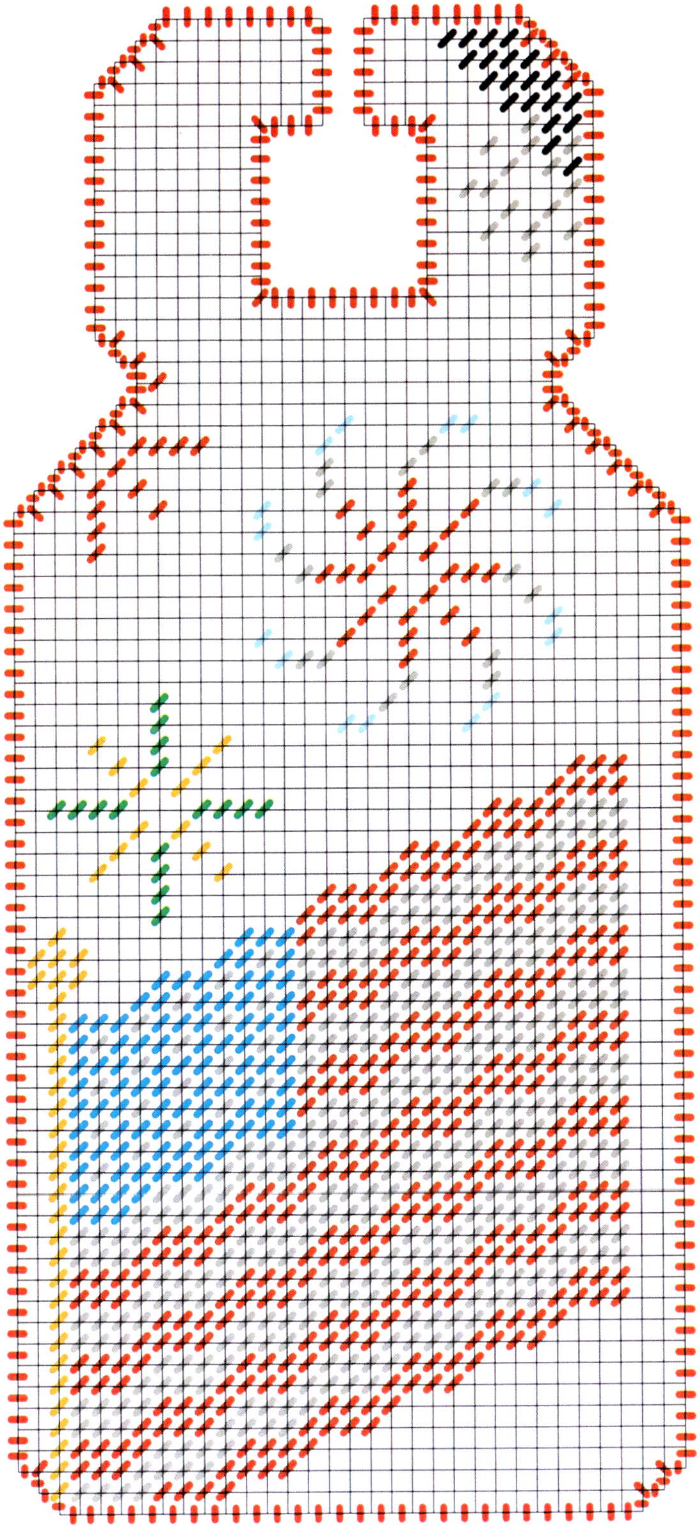

JULY

Color Key

- black
- red
- green
- blue
- lt blue
- white
- yellow

August (33 x 71 threads)

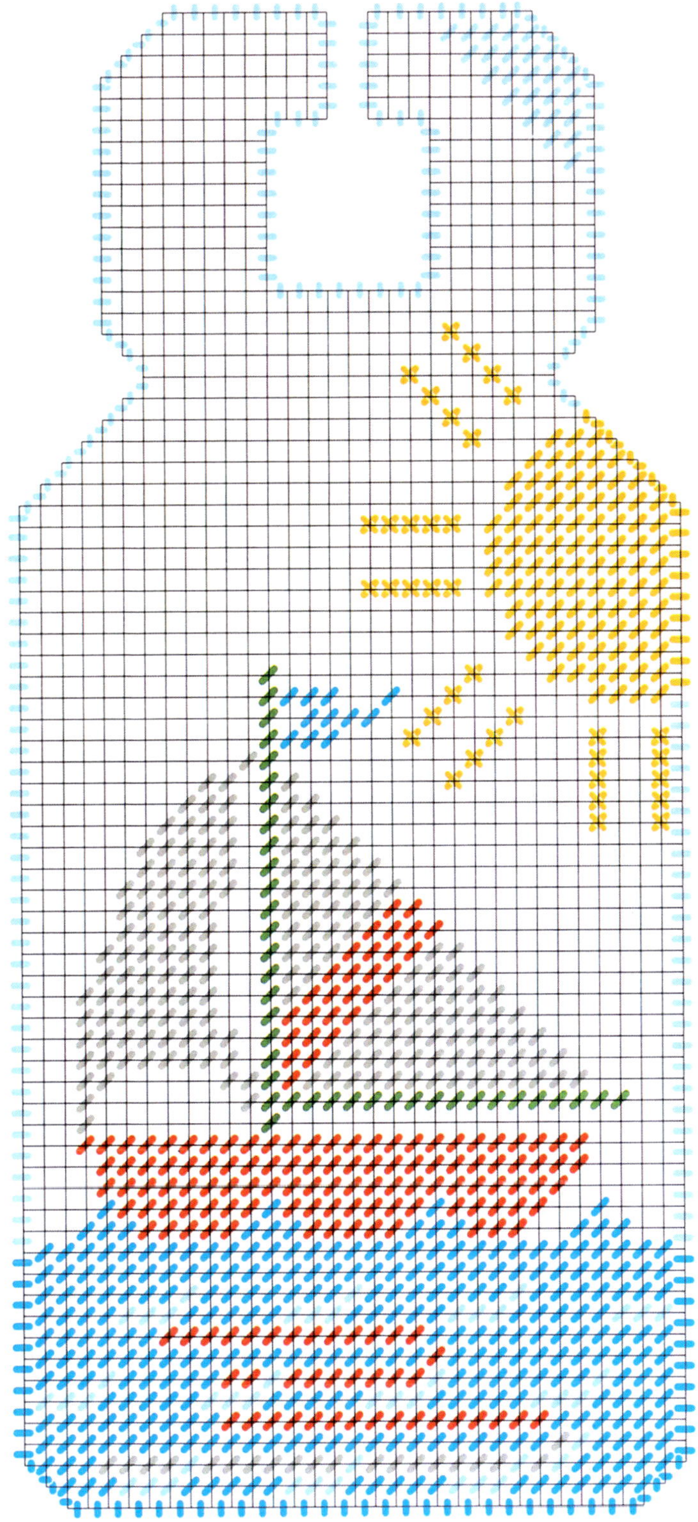

AUGUST

Color Key

- red
- brown
- blue
- lt blue
- white
- yellow

SEPTEMBER

Color Key

- lt brown
- brown
- dk yellow
- lt green
- green
- white
- yellow

September (33 x 71 threads)

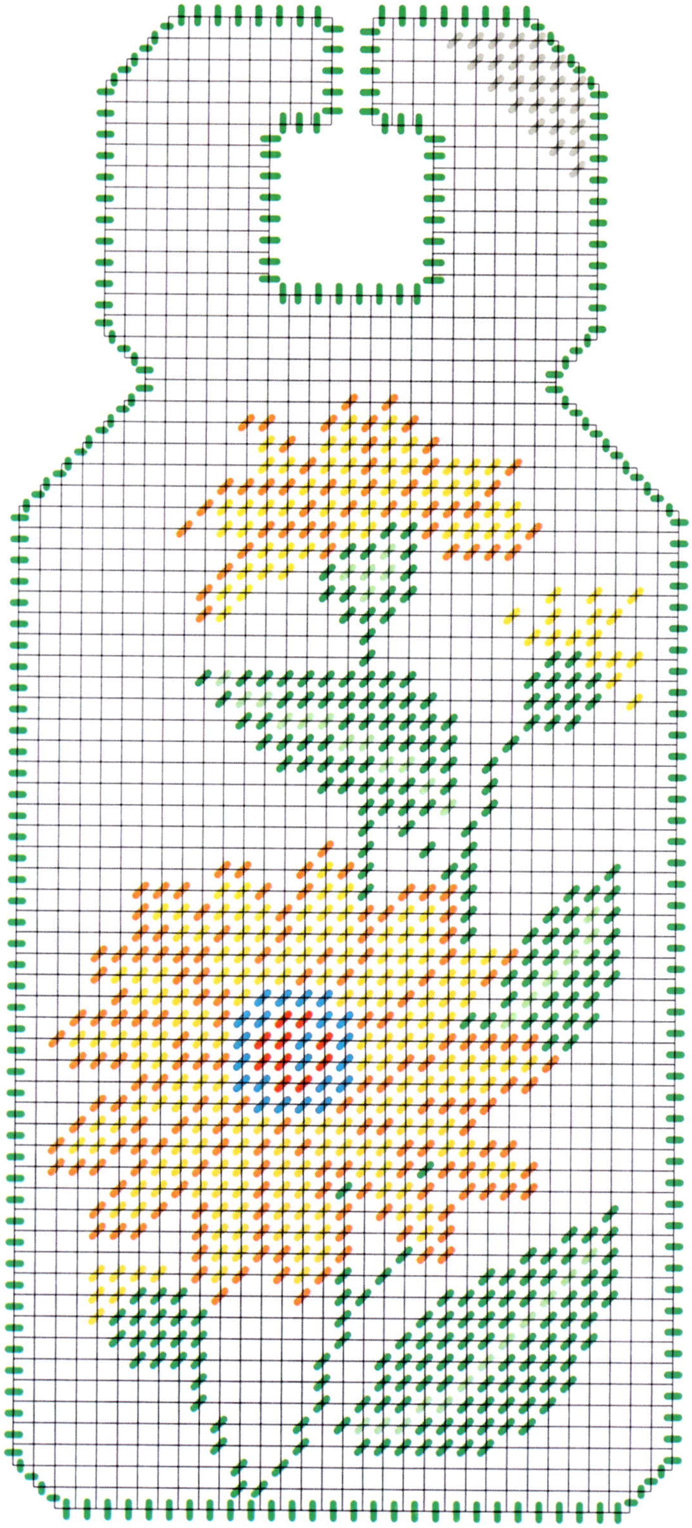

OCTOBER

Color Key

- black
- pink
- yellow
- grey
- white
- dk orange
- dk yellow
- orange
- yellow embroidery floss
- pink embroidery floss
- ecru embroidery floss

October Tail (11 x 22 threads)

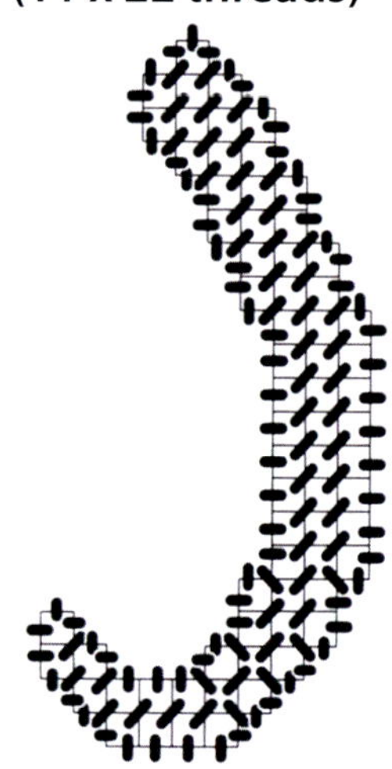

October (33 x 71 threads)

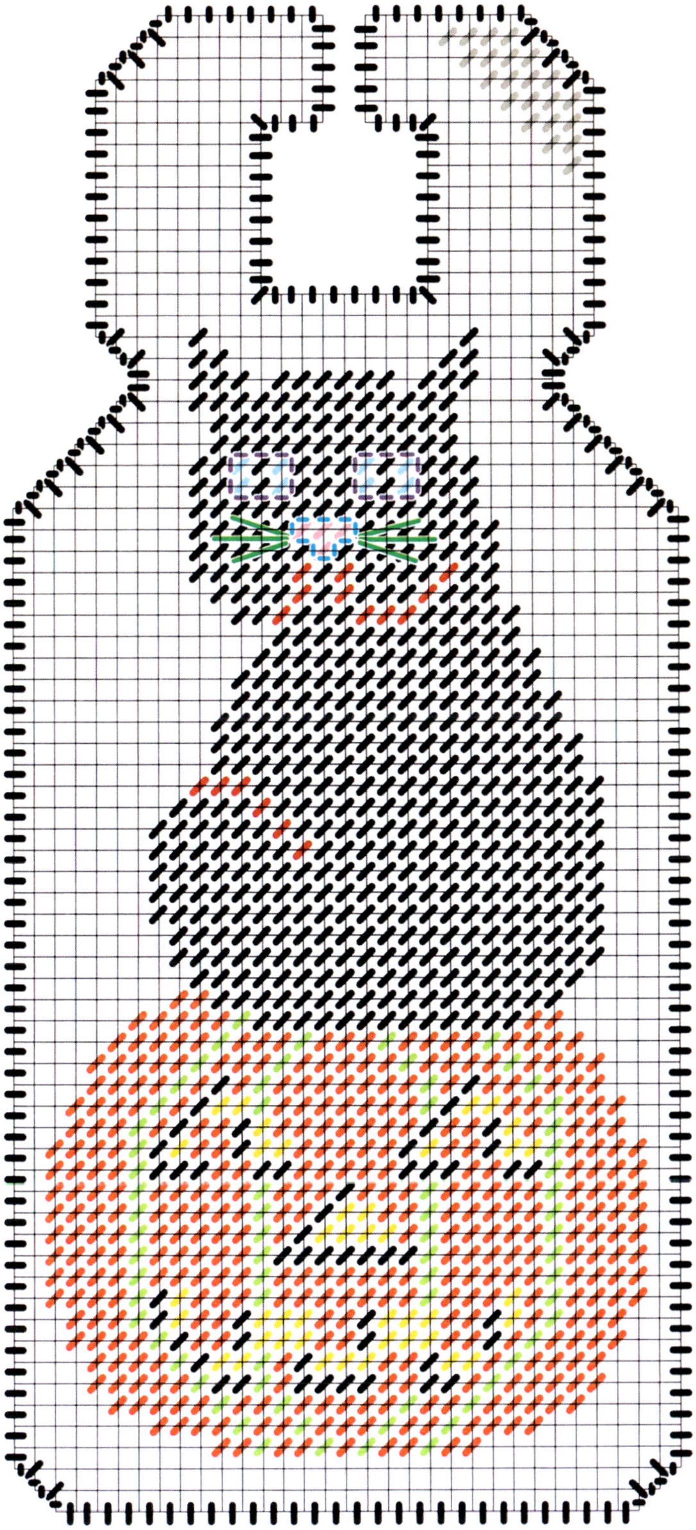

NOVEMBER

Color Key

- lt brown
- brown
- lt green
- green
- white
- dk orange
- orange

November (33 x 71 threads)

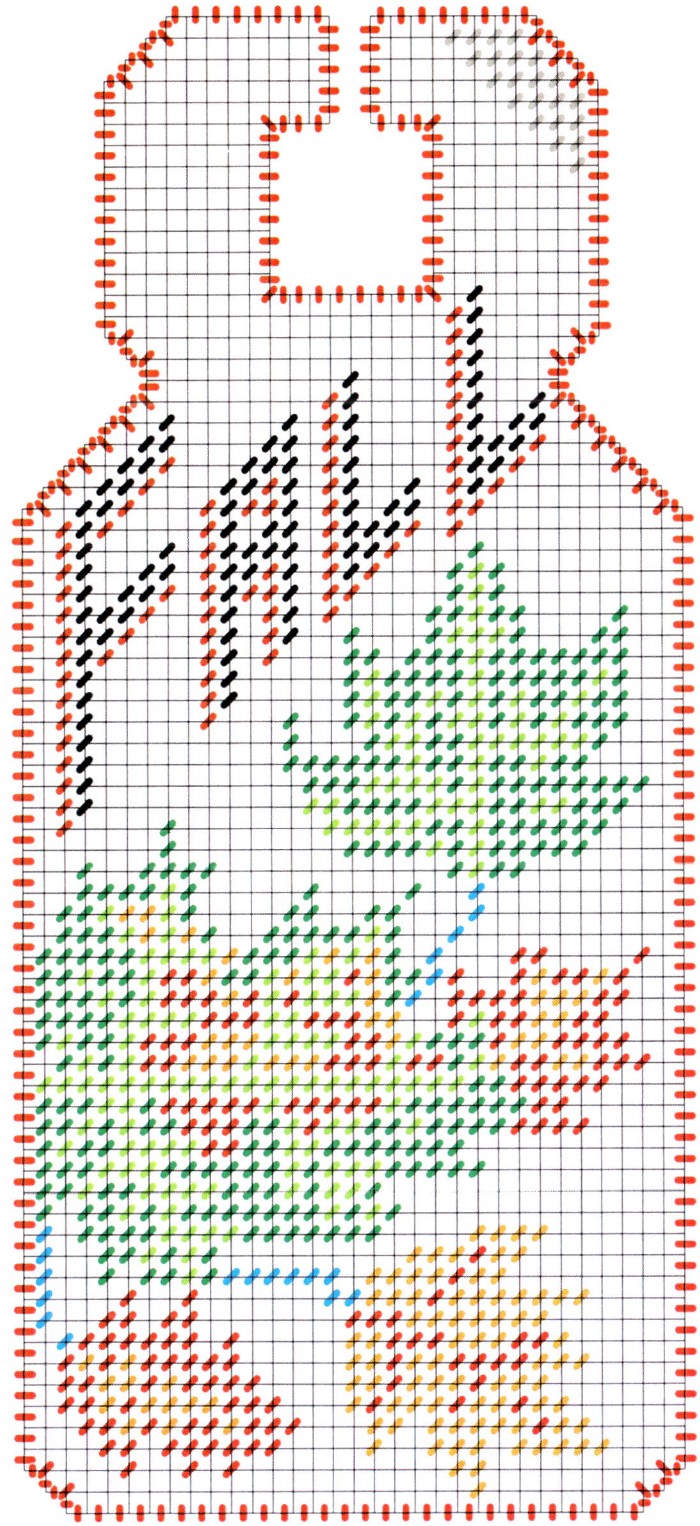

DECEMBER

Color Key
- black
- red
- brown
- green
- dk green
- white
- ○ gold Fringe Stitch

December (33 x 71 threads)

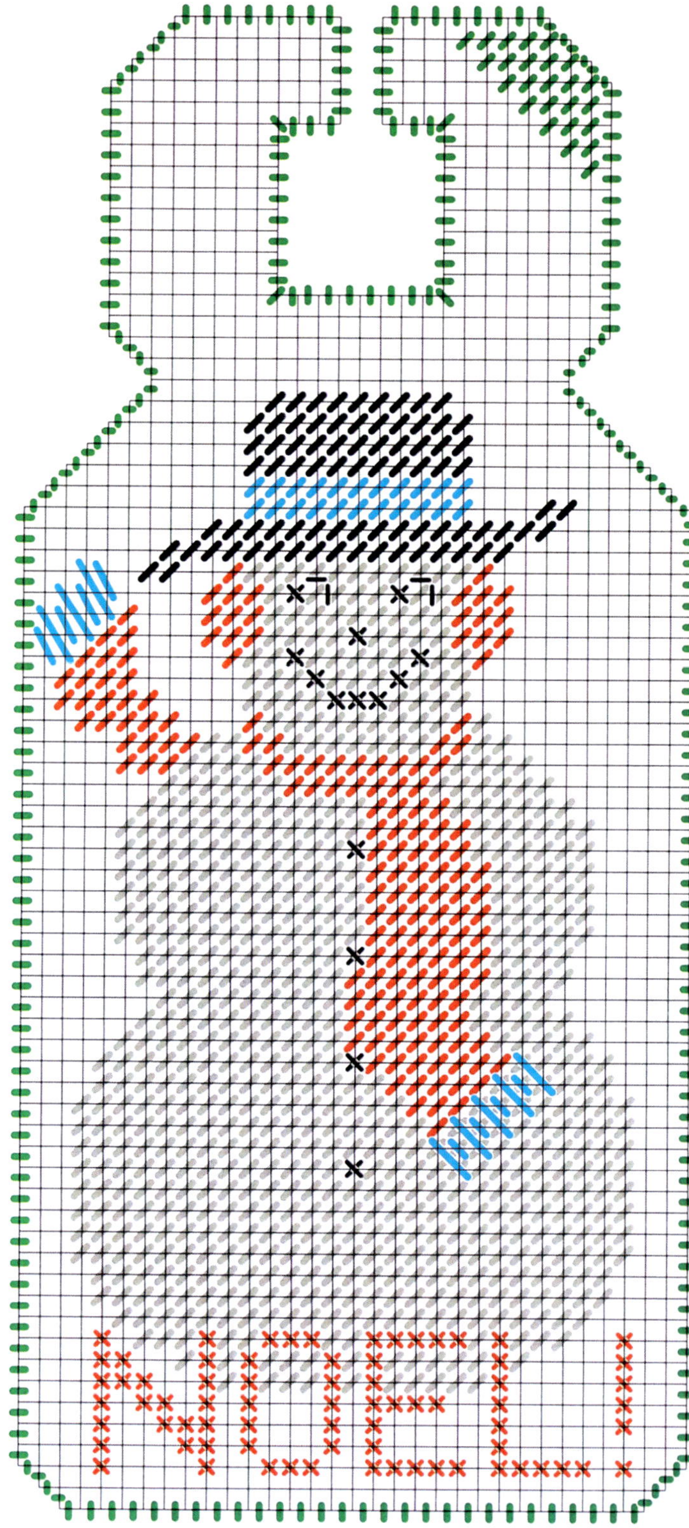

December Arm (work 2)

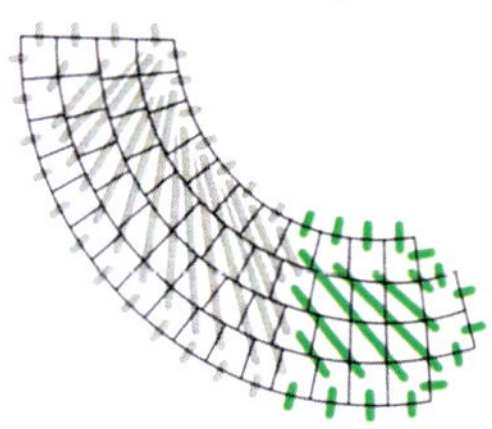

December Broom (7 x 28 threads)

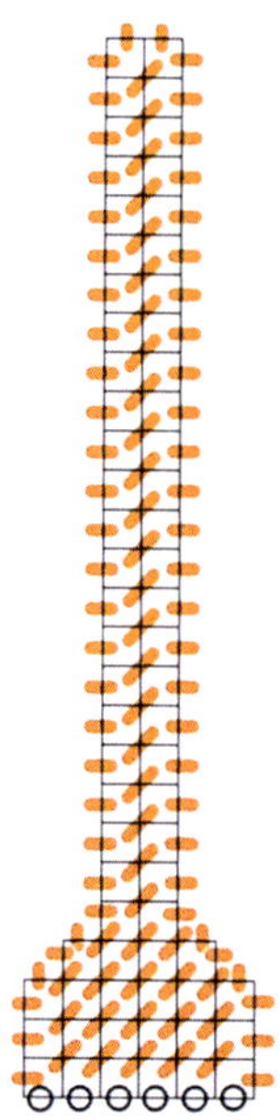

General Instructions

Working with Plastic Canvas

Counting Threads. The lines of the canvas are referred to as threads. Before cutting out the pieces, note the thread count of each chart listed above the chart, indicating the number of threads in the width and height. To cut plastic canvas pieces accurately, count **threads** (not **holes**) as shown in **Fig. 1**.

Fig. 1

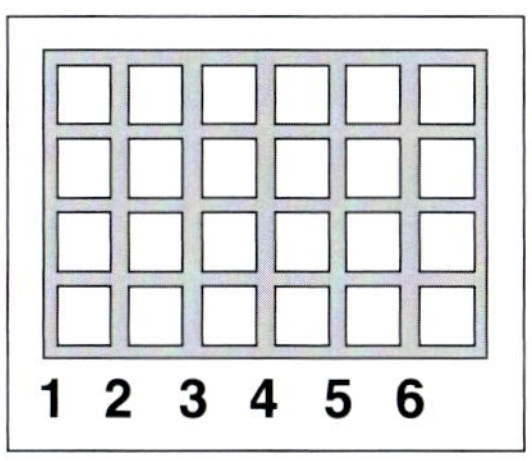

Marking the Canvas. You may use an overhead projector pen to mark the canvas. Outline shape with pen, cut out shape, and remove markings before stitching.

Cutting the Canvas. Cut as close to the thread as possible without cutting into the thread. If you don't cut close enough, "nubs" or "pickets" will be left on the edge. Make sure to cut all nubs from the canvas before stitching because nubs will snag the yarn and are difficult to cover. A craft knife is helpful when cutting a small area from the center of a larger piece of canvas. When using a craft knife, protect the table below with a layer of cardboard.

When cutting canvas along a diagonal, cut through the center of each intersection. This will leave enough plastic canvas on both sides of the cut so that both pieces may be used. Properly cut diagonal corners will be less likely to snag yarn and are easier to cover.

Working with Yarn

Most brands of medium weight yarn have plies which are twisted together to form one strand. When the instructions indicate two plies of yarn, separate the strand of yarn and stitch using only one or two of the plies.

Reading the Color Key

A color key is included for each project, indicating the color used for each stitch on the chart. Additional information may also be included, such as the number of plies to use when working a particular stitch.

Reading the Chart

When possible, the drawing on the chart looks like the completed stitch. For example, the tent stitches on the chart are drawn diagonally across an intersection of threads just as they look on the piece. When a stitch cannot be clearly drawn on the chart, like a French Knot, a symbol will be used instead.

Stitching the Design

Securing the First and Last Stitches. Don't knot the end of your yarn before you begin stitching. Instead, begin each length of yarn by coming up from the wrong side of the canvas and leaving a 1"-2" tail on the wrong side. Hold this tail against the canvas and work the first few stitches over the tail. When secure, clip the tail close to the stitched piece. Long tails can become tangled in future stitches or can show through to the right side of the canvas. After all the stitches of one color in an area are complete, end by running the needle under several stitches on the back. Trim the end close to the stitched piece.

Using Even Tension. Keep your stitching tension consistent, with each stitch lying flat and even. Pulling or yanking the yarn causes the tension to be too tight, and you will be able to see through your project. If the tension is too loose, the stitches won't lie flat. Most stitches tend to twist yarn. Drop your needle and let the yarn untwist occasionally.

Joining Pieces

Straight Edges. To join two or more pieces along a straight edge, place one piece on top of the other with right or wrong sides together. Make sure the edges are even, then overcast the pieces together through all layers.

Shaded Areas. Shaded areas usually mean that all the stitches in that area are used to join pieces of canvas. Do not work these stitches until the project instructions say you should.

Tacking. To tack pieces, run your needle under the backs of some stitches on one stitched piece to secure the yarn. Then run the needle through the canvas or under stitches on the piece to be tacked in place. This should securely attach pieces without tacking stitches showing.

Uneven Edges. When you join a diagonal edge to a straight edge, the holes will not line up exactly. Keep the pieces even and stitch through the holes as many times as necessary to completely cover the canvas.

Stitch Diagrams

*Unless otherwise indicated, bring needle up at **1** and all **odd** numbers and down at **2** and all **even** numbers.*

Alternating Scotch Stitch

This Scotch Stitch variation is worked over a number of threads forming alternating blocks as shown in **Fig. 2**.

Fig. 2

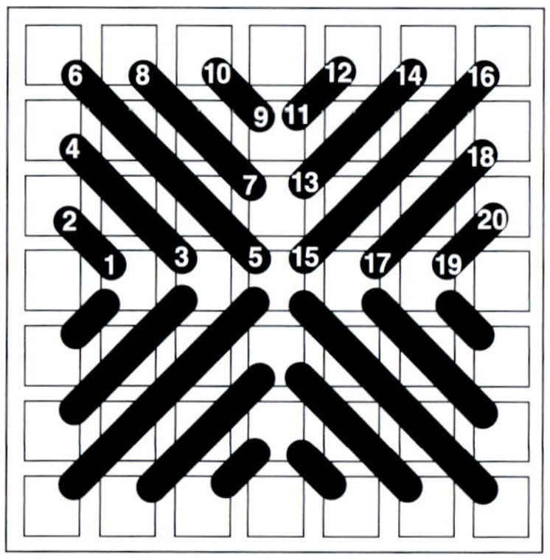

Backstitch

This stitch is worked over completed stitches to outline or define **(Fig. 3)**. It is sometimes worked over more than one thread. It can also be used to cover canvas **(Fig. 4)**.

Fig. 3

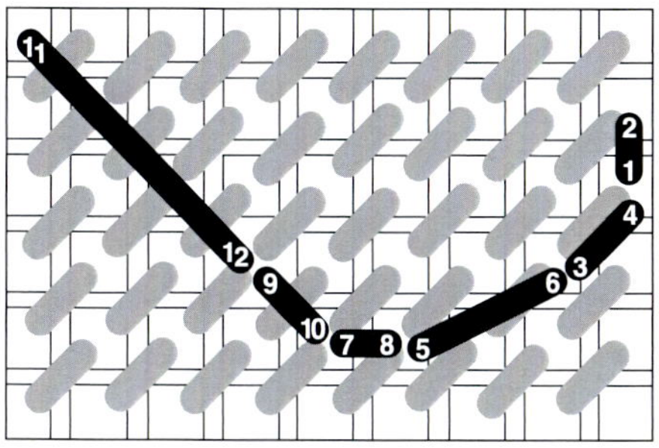

Fig. 4

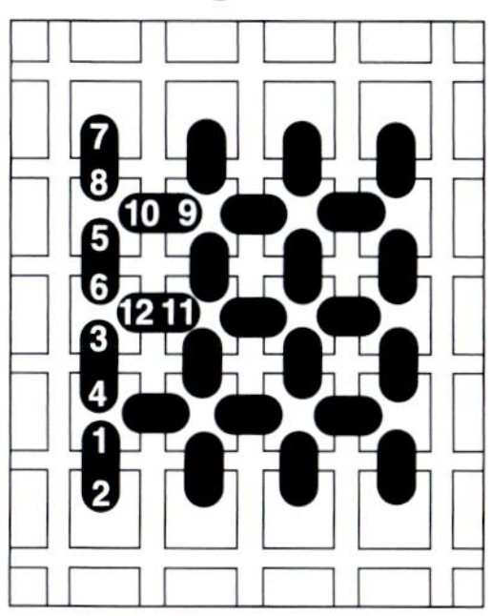

Bargello Stitch

This stitch is a repeated combination of stitches that form a wave pattern. Bargello stitches can be worked either vertically or horizontally and over any number of threads **(Fig. 5)**.

Fig. 5

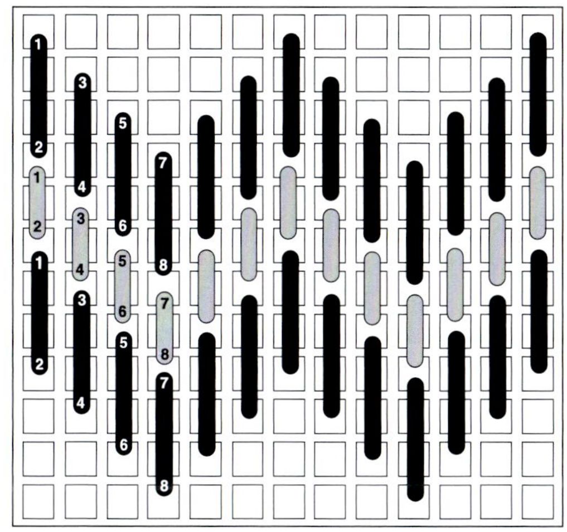

Cross Stitch

This stitch is composed of two stitches **(Fig. 6)**. Cross the top leg of each stitch in the same direction. The number of intersections may vary according to the chart.

Fig. 6

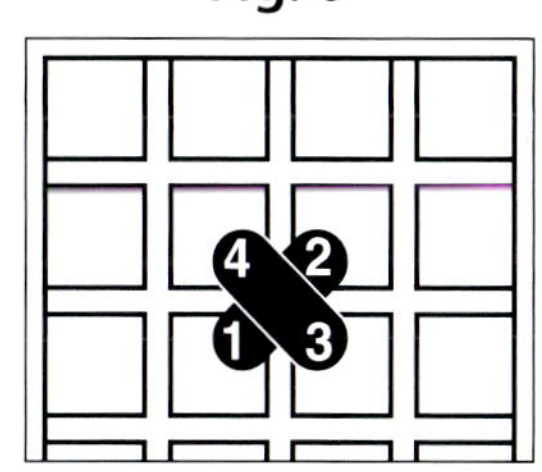

Diagonal Mosaic Stitch

A variation of the Mosaic Stitch, this stitch is worked in diagonal rows as shown in **Fig. 7**.

Fig. 7

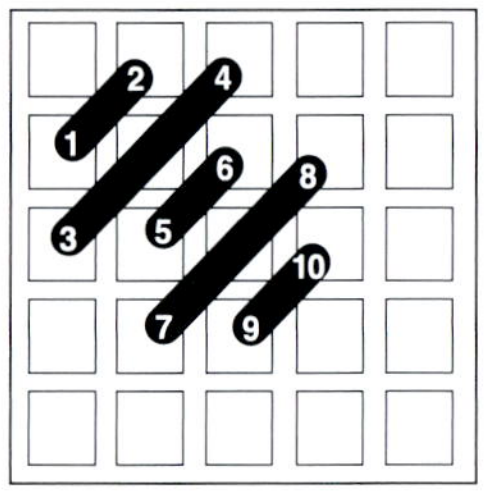

French Knot

Come up at 1. Wrap yarn once around needle. Insert the needle at 2 and pull it through the canvas, holding the yarn until it must be released **(Fig. 8)**.

Fig. 8

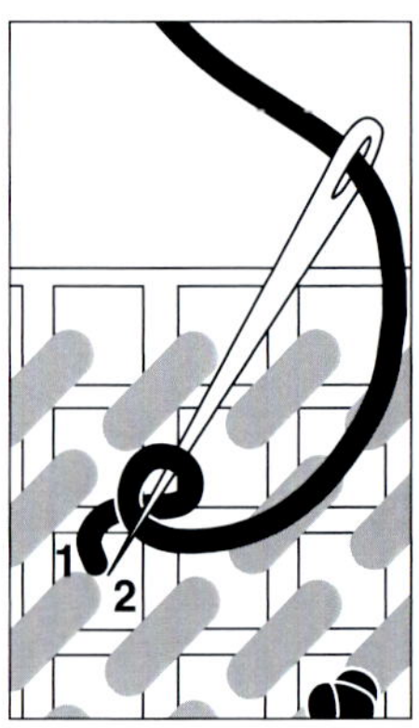

Double French Knot

Bring needle up through hole. Wrap yarn twice around needle and insert needle in same hole, holding end of yarn with non-stitching fingers **(Fig. 9)**. Tighten the knot; then pull needle through canvas, holding yarn until it must be released.

Fig. 9

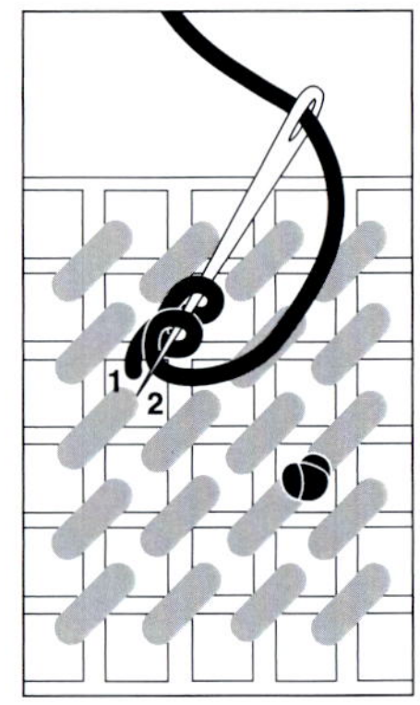

Fringe Stitch

Fold a length of yarn in half. Thread needle with loose ends of yarn. Bring needle up at 1, leaving a 1" loop on the back of the canvas. Bring needle around the edge of canvas and through loop (**Fig. 10**). Pull to tighten loop (**Fig. 11**). Trim fringe to desired length. A dot of glue on back of fringe will help keep stitch in place.

Fig. 10

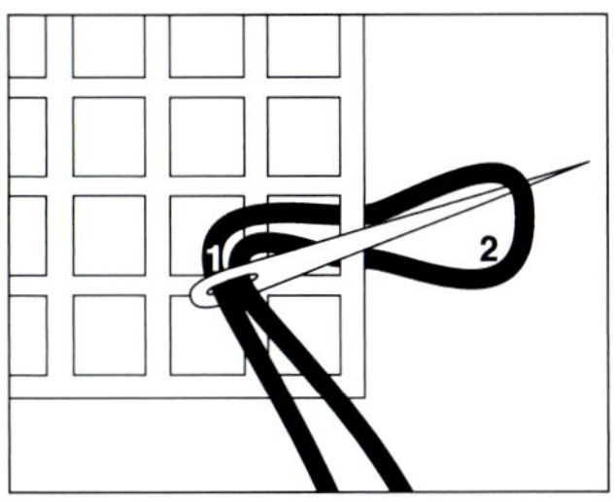

Fig. 11

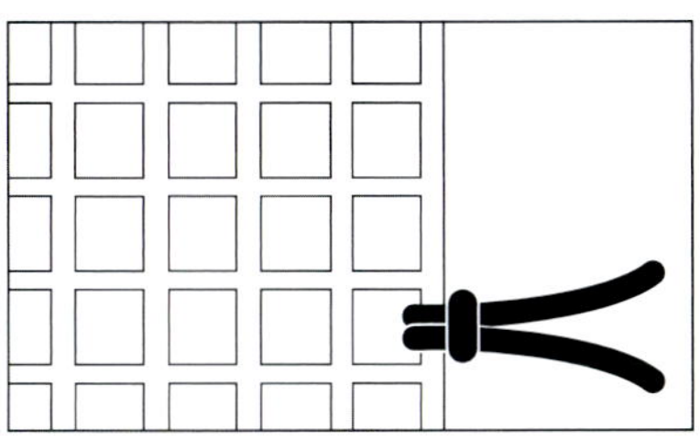

Gobelin Stitch

This straight stitch is worked over two or more threads or intersections (**Fig. 12**). The number of threads or intersections may vary according to the chart.

Fig. 12

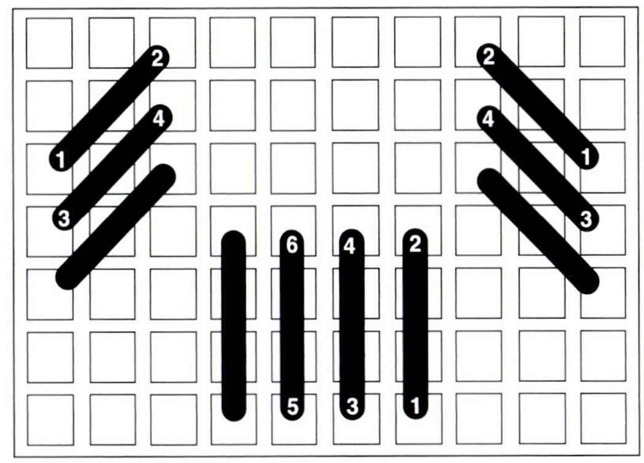

Lazy Daisy Stitch

Work Lazy Daisy stitches last. Bring needle up at 1, make a loop and go down at 1 again (**Fig. 13**). Come up at 2, keeping yarn below the needle's point. Pull needle through and secure loop by bringing yarn over loop and going down at 2.

Fig. 13

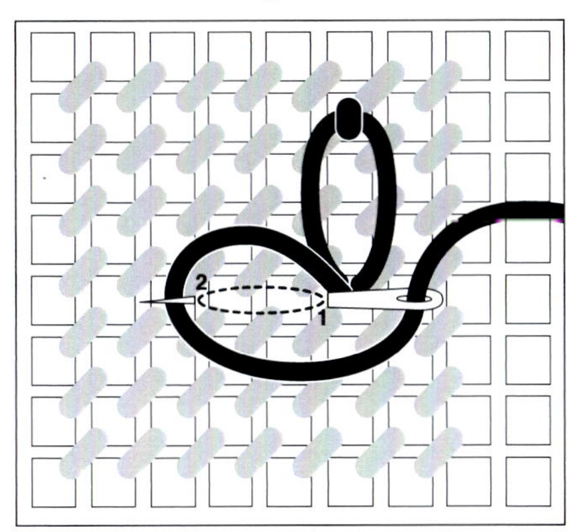

Overcast Stitch

This stitch covers the edge of canvas and joins pieces **(Fig. 14)**. It may be necessary to go through the same hole more than once to get even coverage on the edge, especially at the corners.

Fig. 14

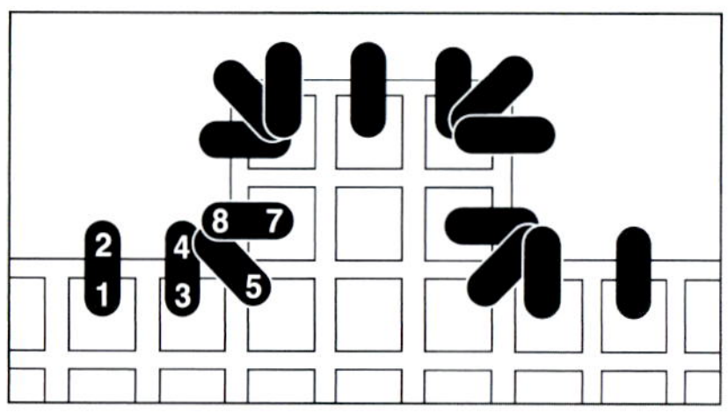

Scotch Stitch

This series of slanted stitches forms squares (**Fig. 15**).

Fig. 15

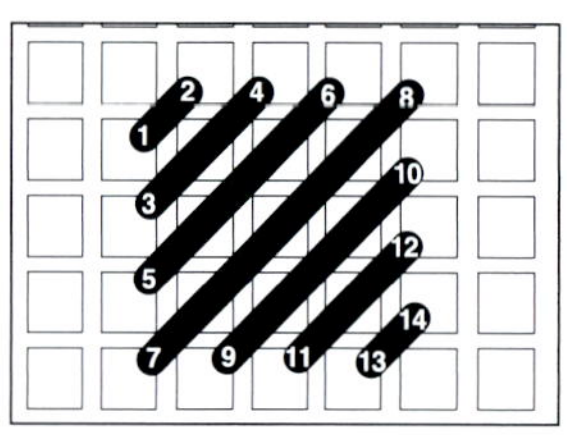

Tent Stitch

This stitch is worked in horizontal or vertical rows over one intersection **(Fig. 16)**. Refer to **Fig. 17** to work the reversed tent stitch.

Fig.16

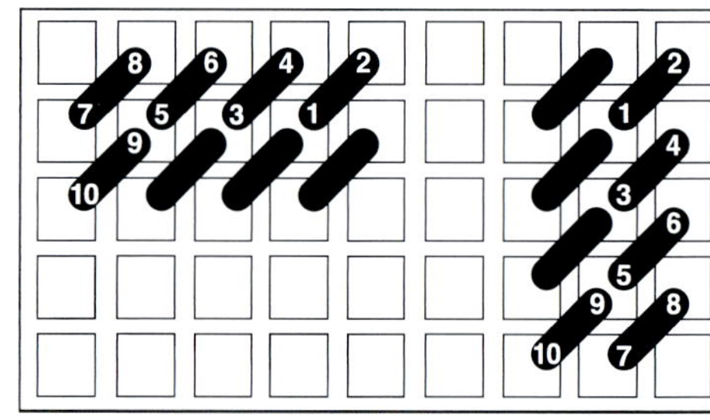

Fig. 17

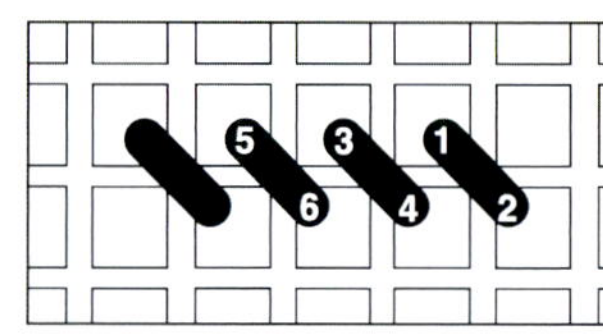

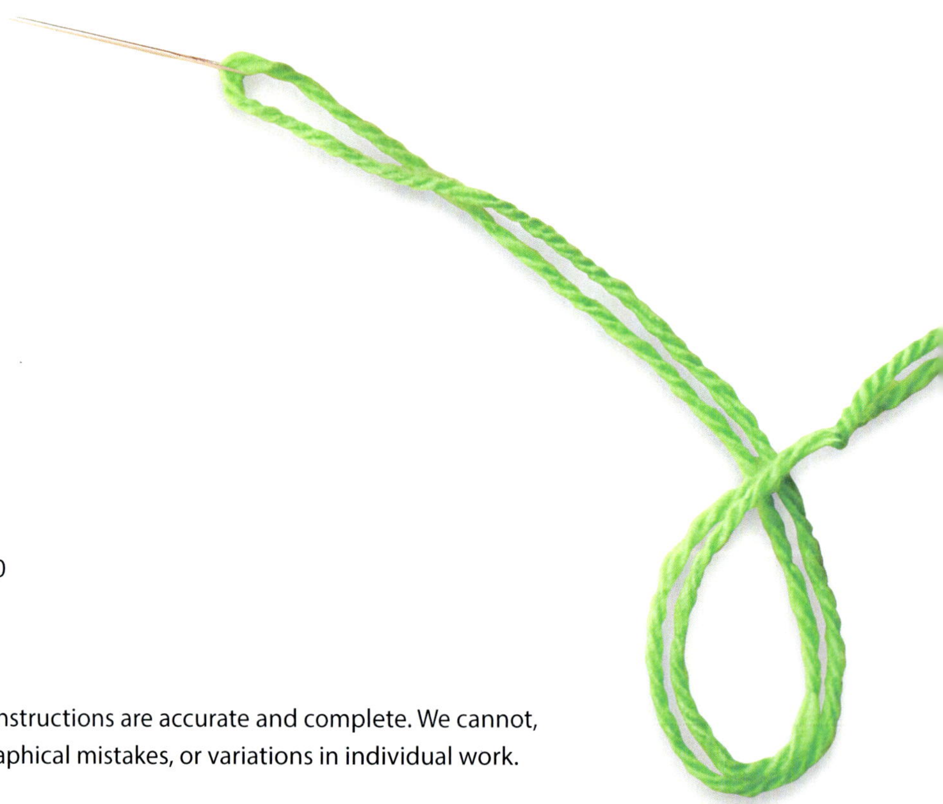

Library of Congress Control Number: 2019933130

Made in U.S.A.

We have made every effort to ensure that these instructions are accurate and complete. We cannot, however, be responsible for human error, typographical mistakes, or variations in individual work.